ANGUS CALDER worked for many
since early retirement in 1993 h:
Ed:

19
is
ed
in
W
of
col
Ar
19
Af

BE
'Li

All ro
Ex-Ser

The Souls of the Dead are Taking the Best Seats

50 World Poets on War

compiled and with an introduction and commentaries by

ANGUS CALDER
and
BETH JUNOR

Luath Press Limited

EDINBURGH

www.luath.co.uk

First Published 2004

The paper used in this book is recyclable. It is made from low
chlorine pulps produced in a low energy, low emission manner from
renewable forests.

Printed and bound by
DigiSource (GB) Ltd., Livingston

Typeset in 10.5 Sabon by S. Fairgrieve 0131 658 1763

dedicated to the memory of
Hamish Henderson

Contents

TWO: 1914–1945

THREE: SINCE 1945

FOUR: RETROSPECTIVE

Introduction

THERE CAN HAVE BEEN no time in the history of Homo Sapiens when song and dance were not part of war. When the Homeric poems were compiled in Greece is uncertain – 7th or 6th centuries BCE. They certainly drew on much earlier oral traditions, of varying date. But the compiler or compilers of the version of the *Iliad* known today established almost at the outset of the Western tradition of written verse that the Epic, along with Tragedy, was the noblest of forms. And the many epics produced since in many countries have invariably involved war, even if 'Homer's' great Roman successor Virgil tilted the form somewhat towards pacification and Camões, sixteenth century poet of the new Portuguese Empire which was already entering into relative decline, brooded uneasily about conflict. *Human Landscapes*, by Turkey's major modern poet Nazim Hikmet, which can be described as an epic in this same sense, shows the persistent appeal of this high mode.

In the huge realm of the Emperor of China, and the vast and multifarious sub-continent of India, war and poetry likewise were symbiotic in ancient times. If nothing in the West could match the scale of vast war presented in the *Mahabharata*, it was also true that no Western poet could comment as subtly as the young Li He, travelling on China's northern frontier, on the sadness of perpetual conflict there. Recent translations from the Old Tamil have given us the *Puṟanāṉūṟu* – literally 'The Four Hundred Poems About the Exterior' – a testament from pre-Aryan India in which poets describe every aspect of the incessant warfare of that period. Meanwhile European counterparts from communities with oral traditions and scribes struck up themes of war, as in the Anglo-Saxon *Beowulf* and later English and Scottish ballads. In Elizabeth I's England as in Virgil's Rome there was an inkling that war and society could be separated – aristocrats built big houses which were not castles. But then Europe plunged into its Thirty Years War and the eighteenth and nineteenth centuries saw alternations between specious peace and periods when whole populations, as before, were engulfed in war. This, however, had long since become a specialised, rather than commonplace theme of Western literature, just as fighting in the developing nation-states was left to specialised soldiers. And so it was that, at least in the West, the twentieth century generated a conception of 'War Poetry' implying novelty in the fact that the two had come together, when conscription in 1914-1918 (as pre-figured in the US Civil War of 1861-1865) hurled young civilians in their millions into appalling battles.

Both language and war are societal inheritances, not the creation of individuals. Poetry oral or written, or more generally, language is among the defining characteristics of what it is to be 'human'. As a species, for all that we have achieved through our faculty of language, far from using this tool for thought as a means to overcome our propensity for war, we have used it to develop and refine ever more 'efficient' killing practices. Once, boasting about warlike deeds was the chief job of bards. Now many, it seems most, who return from war don't or cannot recount their experiences – a gulf has widened between fighter and civilian. War, like all forms of oppression, depends for its subsistence on premeditated or uncon-scious impoverishment of language. War depletes language; poetry enriches and refreshes language and good war poetry breaks silence, restoring voice to those who have experienced horrors that lie beyond the language of everyday discourse. Leaving aside the interesting question whether war movies (increasingly shocking in their 'realistic' re-enactments) actually help those who watch them to any greater understanding of the physical and ethical horrors of conflict than the old conventions of Westerns or such fantasies as Lord of the Rings, we are clear that poetry has a special role. We hope that the poetry we've selected illuminates the impact of war on the humanity of all concerned, including the combatants themselves, in ways that even the best prose rarely can. We must wait in expectation, as a society, for more poets, including soldier poets, of the wars we witness today to emerge, for the combatant's own sake as much as for the soul of this age in which we live. Mahmoud Darwish's 'State of Siege' is included here as one of the finest contemporary examples from life in a military-controlled region. Not even the increasing use of drugs or sound blasting into soldiers' helmets can numb humanity to the profundity of war experiences. One of the senses will imprint that experience on the unconscious, to emerge if only as in Louis Simpson's case, as a kind of automatic writing later recognised as one's own war experience. We *expect* this poetry of the future – this collection also communicates to today's combatants and civilians affected by war that people are prepared to listen, again.

We have given quite small space to the 'Soldier Poets' of the First World War, much more to writing from World War II in which civilians from Belfast to Moscow, from Darwin, Australia, to Tokyo, Japan, were targeted by aerial bombardment, and the genocide of Jewish people by Nazis was, hideously, by far the largest, but not the only instance of its kind. Wars, with ever more sophisticated weaponry, have since gone on like that. The warfare which is now, through TV, an everyday part of the luckiest, most peaceful life, *in situ* spares no one in its path and one commanding case for good poetry is that it can resensitise its readers to the nature of the horrors they glimpse this way.

Poetry's ability to suspend events, to slow down an image and draw attention to the detail and human experience of war is of inestimable value in this information age, serving to re-train our minds and responses to war statistics. The voice of poetry is intimate. The voice we hear in our minds when we read may be our own, so that poetry grafts experience to us, dissolving detachment, akin to the way in which music moves us. When dialect is used, the voice of another may enter us. Kipling is particularly powerful this way, and his 'Ford O' Kabul River', included here, is a fine example. Good war poetry narrows the distance between media reports and our own homes and values. In this sense poetry completes the war record.

Information has an allure in itself and can seduce us into thinking that 'facts' alone give us knowledge of war. Without its poetry, our understanding of any war is limited to specifics of date, time, location, propagandist numbers of combatant and civilian casualties, descriptions of tactics employed and weaponry used. Poetry records the essence of an event independent of its factual details:

Day and month? Like an echo, the mountains:
'The day the Czechs fell to the Germans.'
– Marina Tsvetayeva, 'An Officer'

As Tsevtayeva has done here, we've thought it necessary to provide only enough information to place the poems in context. Anything beyond that can be looked up. In his acceptance speech for the Nobel Prize for Literature, Odysseus Elytis said that poetry 'stands for the only space where the power of number does not count'. In our selection women and men from the very young to the old, combatant and civilian, lover, parent, son, and in Soyinka and Klikovac's examples, ghosts of the war dead are all represented. An appalling theme is the sameness of individual experience across such a wide range of contexts and time.

None of the poems here serves any immediate political purpose and this is partly what makes them good examples of their craft. That is, they are non-aligned records of human experience, illuminations of detail, objects of art unifying humanity. They are time given us to observe and reflect upon war's effects. Torrents of bad poetry protesting against war have been released in the West in the last nine or ten decades, and we would stress that crude verse inveighing against militarism is no more sensitising than patriotic rhetoric. Such invective serves temporary political uses. John Cornford wrote blatantly propagandist essays but this does not affect his best poetry.

Good poetry, in Auden's fine but easily misunderstood formulation in 'In Memory of W. B. Yeats', 'makes nothing happen' in the way that bombs and media lies make things happen – instantly, temporarily. It 'survives in the valley of its making'.

If almost no poet can hope to match the combination of virtuosity with passion found in Celan's 'Death Fugue' and Lowell's 'For the Union Dead', we hope we provide forty-eight other examples which have survived, or will survive, in the valleys of their making.

AC, BJ
Edinburgh, August 2004

14

ONE: BATTLES LONG AGO

Bible

David Mourns Jonathan

King David is supposed to have reigned in Palestine c 1000 BCE. He succeeded Saul, whose son Jonathan had been his dearest friend. In the Bible, at the beginning of the Second Book of Samuel, news comes to David that Saul and Jonathan have died fighting Israel's longstanding Philistine enemies. For problems of dating 'Samuel' and assessing the historicity of this and other Biblical texts, see Robin Lane Fox, THE UNAUTHORISED VERSION: TRUTH AND FICTION IN THE BIBLE *(1991). What is certain is that the Authorised Version of the Bible in English, commissioned by James VI and I and published in 1611, makes something unforgettable of David's grief.*

And David lamented with this lamentation over Saul and over Jonathan his son...

The beauty of Israel is slain upon thy high places: how are the mighty fallen!

Tell it not in Gath, publish it not in the streets of Askelon; lest the daughters of the Philistines rejoice, lest the daughters of the uncircumcised triumph.

Ye mountains of Gilboa, let there be no dew, neither let there be rain, upon you, nor fields of offerings: for there the shield of the mighty is vilely cast away, the shield of Saul, as though he had not been anointed with oil.

From the blood of the slain, from the fat of the mighty, the bow of Jonathan turned not back, and the sword of Saul returned not empty.

Saul and Jonathan were lovely and pleasant in their lives, and in their death they were not divided: they were swifter than eagles, they were stronger than lions.

Ye daughters of Israel, weep over Saul, who clothed you in
scarlet, with other delights, who put on ornaments of gold
upon your apparel.

How are the mighty fallen in the midst of the battle! O
Jonathan, thou wast slain in thine high places.

I am distressed for thee, my brother Jonathan: very pleasant hast
thou been unto me: thy love to me was wonderful, passing
the love of women.

How are the mighty fallen, and the weapons of war perished!

Homer (c. 700 BCE)

The Return of Hector's Corpse to Troy

The tale of the ten-year long siege of Troy by Greek chieftains is legendary, not factual, and whatever actual incidents might have inspired it occurred centuries before the ILIAD *was written down – according to tradition by one poet, Homer. The epic gathers together oral traditions, and shapes them round the 'wrath of Achilles', near the end of the siege. The greatest Greek fighter, at the outset of the poem, is at odds with their general, Agamemnon, and refuses to fight. When his dearest friend Patroclus dies in battle, Achilles returns to the fray berserk with craving for vengeance. He slaughters many Trojans and at last kills his prime target, the greatest Trojan hero, Hector. In a deeply moving scene, Hector's father, King Priam of Troy, comes secretly to Achilles's tent at night to beg for his son's body so that it can receive proper burial. Achilles agrees, and the body goes back to Troy. This concluding passage of the* ILIAD *is translated by Robert Fagles.*

Once they reached the ford where the river runs clear,
the strong, whirling Xanthus sprung of immortal Zeus,
Hermes went his way to the steep heights of Olympus
as Dawn flung out her golden robe across the earth,
and the two men, weeping, groaning, drove the team
toward Troy and the mules brought on the body.
No one saw them at first, neither man nor woman,
none before Cassandra, golden as goddess Aphrodite.
She had climbed to Pergamus heights and from that point
she saw her beloved father swaying tall in the chariot,
flanked by the herald, whose cry could rouse the city.
And Cassandra saw *him* too . . .
drawn by the mules and stretched out on his bier.
She screamed and her scream rang out through all Troy:
'Come, look down, you men of Troy, you Trojan women!

Behold Hector now – if you ever once rejoiced
to see him striding home, home alive from battle!
He was the greatest joy of Troy and all our people!'

Her cries plunged Troy into uncontrollable grief
and not a man or woman was left inside the walls.
They streamed out at the gates to meet Priam
bringing in the body of the dead. Hector –
his loving wife and noble mother were first
to fling themselves on the wagon rolling on,
the first to tear their hair, embrace his head
and a wailing throng of people milled around them.
And now, all day long till the setting sun went down
they would have wept for Hector there before the gates
if the old man, steering the car, had not commanded,
'Let me through with the mules! Soon, in a moment,
you can have your fill of tears – once I've brought him home.'

So he called and the crowds fell back on either side,
making way for the wagon. Once they had borne him
into the famous halls, they laid his body down
on his large carved bed and set beside him singers
to lead off the laments, and their voices rose in grief –
they lifted the dirge high as the women wailed in answer.
And white-armed Andromache led their songs of sorrow,
cradling the head of Hector, man-killing Hector
gently in her arms: 'O my husband
cut off from life so young! You leave me a widow,
lost in the royal halls – and the boy only a baby,
the son we bore together, you and I so doomed.
I cannot think he will ever come to manhood.
Long before *that* the city will be sacked,
plundered top to bottom! Because you are dead,
her great guardian, you who always defended Troy,
who kept her loyal wives and helpless children safe,
all who will soon be carried off in the hollow ships
and I with them –

And you, my child, will follow me
to labor, somewhere, at harsh, degrading work,
slaving under some heartless master's eye – that,
or some Achaean marauder will seize you by the arm
and hurl you headlong down from the ramparts – horrible death –
enraged at you because Hector once cut down his brother,
his father or his son, yes, hundreds of armed Achaeans
gnawed the dust of the world, crushed by Hector's hands!
Your father, remember, was no man of mercy . . .
not in the horror of battle, and that is why
the whole city of Troy mourns you now, my Hector –
you've brought your parents accursed tears and grief
but to me most of all you've left the horror, the heartbreak!
For you never died in bed and stretched your arms to me
or said some last word from the heart I can remember,
always, weeping for you through all my nights and days!'

Her voice rang out in tears and the women wailed in answer
and Hecuba led them now in a throbbing chant of sorrow:
'Hector, dearest to me by far of all my sons . . .
and dear to the gods while we still shared this life –
and they cared about you still, I see, even after death.
Many the sons I had whom the swift runner Achilles
caught and shipped on the barren salt sea as slaves
to Samos, to Imbros, to Lemnos shrouded deep in mist!
But you, once he slashed away your life with his brazen spear
he dragged you time and again around his comrade's tomb,
Patroclus whom you killed – not that he brought Patroclus
back to life by that. But I have you with me now...
Fresh as the morning dew you lie in the royal halls
like one whom Apollo, lord of the silver bow,
has approached and shot to death with gentle shafts.'

Her voice rang out in tears and an endless wail rose up
and Helen, the third in turn, led their songs of sorrow:
'Hector! Dearest to me of all my husband's brothers –
my husband, Paris, magnificent as a god ...

he was the one who brought me here to Troy –
Oh how I wish I'd died before that day!
But this, now, is the twentieth year for me
since I sailed here and forsook my own native land,
yet never once did I hear from you a taunt, an insult.
But if someone else in the royal halls would curse me,
one of your brothers or sisters or brothers' wives
trailing their long robes, even your own mother –
not your father, always kind as my own father –
why, you'd restrain them with words, Hector,
you'd win them to my side...
you with your gentle temper, all your gentle words.
And so in the same breath I mourn for you and me,
my doom-struck, harrowed heart! Now there is no one left
in the wide realm of Troy, no friend to treat me kindly –
all the countrymen cringe from me in loathing!'

Her voice rang out in tears and vast throngs wailed
and old King Priam rose and gave his people orders:
'Now, you men of Troy, haul timber into the city!
Have no fear of an Argive ambush packed with danger –
Achilles vowed, when he sent me home from the black ships,
not to do us harm till the twelfth dawn arrives.'

At his command they harnessed oxen and mules to wagons,
they assembled before the city walls with all good speed
and for nine days hauled in a boundless store of timber.
But when the tenth Dawn brought light to the mortal world
they carried gallant Hector forth, streaming tears,
and they placed his corpse aloft the pyre's crest,
flung a torch and set it all aflame.

                    At last,
when young Dawn with her rose-red fingers shone once more,
the people massed around illustrious Hector's pyre.
And once they'd gathered, crowding the meeting grounds,
they first put out the fires with glistening wine,

wherever the flames still burned in all their fury.
Then they collected the white bones of Hector –
all his brothers, his friends-in-arms, mourning,
and warm tears came streaming down their cheeks.
They placed the bones they found in a golden chest,
shrouding them round and round in soft purple cloths.
They quickly lowered the chest in a deep, hollow grave
and over it piled a cope of huge stones closely set,
then hastily heaped a barrow, posted lookouts all around
for fear the Achaean combat troops would launch their attack
before the time agreed. And once they'd heaped the mound
they turned back home to Troy, and gathering once again
they shared a splendid funeral feast in Hector's honor,
held in the house of Priam, king by will of Zeus.

And so the Trojans buried Hector breaker of horses.

Virgil (70–19 BCE)

Fighting through Troy

Virgil (Publius Vergilius Maro) wrote his epic the AENEID *for the first Emperor, Augustus Caesar, who seemed to have brought peace to Rome after terrible civil wars. Its hero Aeneas is a Trojan hero sailing West and destined to prepare the foundation of Rome amid conflict with local Italian peoples. Virgil takes a more critical view of combat than his model, 'Homer'. Here Aeneas, in Carthage, describes to the city's queen, Dido, the dreadful carnage which preceded his escape from Troy, after the Greeks had treacherously entered it through the famous expedient of the Wooden Horse. The translation is by C. Day Lewis.*

That night! – what words can render its deaths and its disaster?
What tears can rise to the level of all that was suffered then?
An ancient city is falling, after long years of power:
So many motionless bodies prostrated everywhere
Along the streets, in the houses, on the gods' holy thresholds.
Not the Trojans alone paid their account in blood:
There were times when courage returned even though we knew
    we were beaten,
And then the conquering Greeks fell. All over the town you saw
Heart-rending agony, panic, and every shape of death.
    The first to cross our path was Androgeos, with a fair-sized
Body of Greeks around him: he thought, in his ignorance,
We were friends, and went so far as to hail us with comradely
    words: –
Get going, men! Whatever has kept you so long? What do you
Mean by this slackness? The rest of the Greeks have been burning
    and sacking
Ilium; and here are you only just turned up from the ships.
    He spoke; and at once – for he got no satisfactory answer –
It dawned on him that the men he'd fallen in with were hostile.

Startled, he brought up sharp, checked speech, winced away.
Like one who, forcing his way through sharp briars, accidentally
Has trod on a snake, and in sudden panic shudders away from
Its angrily-rearing head, its gunmetal neck puffed out –
Androgeos, unnerved at the sight of us, made to retreat.
We went for him and his party, surrounded them; and since
They had no local knowledge and were paralysed with fear
Picked them off one by one. So fortune favoured our first move.
Flown with success and in high spirits, Coroebus exclaimed:–
    Comrades, let's follow up where fortune has first shown us
A way to survival, and play our luck while it is good!
Change shields with these dead Greeks, put on their badges and
    flashes!
Craft or courage – who cares, when an enemy has to be beaten?
The Greeks themselves shall equip us.
                    So saying, he put on
Androgeos' plumed helmet, his shield with its fine heraldic
Device, and fitted onto his side the Argive sword.
Rhipeus, and Dymas too, and all our warriors gleefully
Followed suit, each arming himself from the spoils just taken
Then we went on through the press of the Greeks, under false
    favours
Of alien gods. Many a sharp engagement we fought
In the blindfold night, and many a Greek we despatched to
    Hades.
Some broke and ran for the ships, ran for the sure protection
The beaches gave: one lot, driven by sheer cowardice,
Climbed the horse again and returned to the womb they had
    come from.
    Ah well, there's no trusting the gods for anything, once
    they're against you! –
Over there was Priam's daughter, Cassandra, her hair flying,
Being dragged away from Minerva's house, from its very sanctuary,
Her burning eyes uplifted to heaven, but in vain –
Her eyes, for she could not lift her delicate palms, they were
    pinioned.
Coroebus found this sight too much: in a passion of rage

He bores right into the thick of the foe; he wants to be killed.
We followed him, all of us, attacking in close order.
Now, we were first mown down by the fire of our own side,
    shooting
From the high temple roof; a deplorable slaughter began
Through mistaken identity – our Greek equipment and crests.
Next, the Greeks rallied, shouting with rage at the attempt to
Rescue Cassandra: they went for us – Ajax most vindictively,
And the two sons of Atreus, with the whole battalion of
    Dolopes:
So, when a hurricane breaks, you may get a clash and a tussle
Of winds – the West, the South, and the East wind rough-riding
His orient steeds: then forests whine, and Nereus in wild rage
Churns the sea with his trident and raises it mountains-high.
Many Greeks appeared now – the ones whom, in the confusing
    darkness
Of night, our ruse had routed and stampeded over the town.
These were the first to recognize our shields, our fraudulent
    weapons;
They noticed, too, the foreign tongue which gave us away.
Well, this was it. We were crushed by weight of numbers.
    Coroebus
Went down to Peneleus' sword at the altar of the war-puissant
Goddess; then Rhipeus fell, he who of all the Trojans
Was most fair-minded, the one who was most regardful of justice:
God's ways are inscrutable. Now Hypanis fell and Dymas
Shot by their own friends. And Panthus – not all his goodness
Nor the headband he wore as Apollo's priest saved him from death.
Oh ashes of Ilium! O flames that my world died in!
I call you to witness that I, at your setting, was facing the
    Greeks' fire,
Evading no danger in combat: if fate had meant me to die then
I'd have earned that death by the way I fought.

The Puṟanāṉūṟu

This Classical Tamil collection of 400 poems was written between the 1st and 3rd centuries CE by more than 150 poets, including at least 10 women poets. Poem 112 is said to have been composed for the daughters of Pári, after their father was killed in a siege of his mountain fortress. Poems 253 and 254 refer to the practice of breaking and discarding a woman's bracelets when she is widowed.

The language is Old Tamil, the precursor of modern Tamil and Malayalam, translated by a linguist/poet duo, George Hart and Hank Heifetz.

112

On that day, under the white light of that moon,
we had our father and no enemies had taken the hill.
On this day, under the white light of this moon, the kings,
royal drums beating out the victory,
have taken the hill. And we! we have no father.

253

You do not feel my pain now. Because you have died, I cannot
rejoice with the young men who wear chaplets bound with
    strong cord
as they celebrate. Must I go and tell your people of your death
while I lift my hands empty of bangles, showing whitened bands
as when the bark is stripped from sprouts
of bamboo that have never seeded? Tell me what I must do!

254

The young men and the old men have left for another place.
When I embrace you, young warrior, you do not rise,
with your chest pressing the earth, you who have fallen
in the wilderness! While I show my arms that are pale
and wear no bangles, if the word that their young man is now
only this should reach your family, what will happen
to his mother who praises him every day, ceaselessly
repeating "For me the strength and majesty of my son
are like the fresh fruit growing in front of the city
on a ripe banyan tree that is all
filled with birds"? You should feel deep pity for her!

China's Northern Wars

Li He (790–816)

Song of an Arrowhead from Chang-Ping

Li He was a Chinese poet who was original to the point of eccentricity. This poem is typical of him in its vivid scene painting combined with weird suggestions. The poet visits the site of an ancient battlefield, where in 260 BCE, in the process of unifying China, the forces of Qin were said to have captured and then buried alive 400,000 men of Zhao. In Li He's day, over a thousand years later, farmers were still turning up relics of the massacre. He hears the ghosts of the dead wailing because they were not buried with proper rites and libations. His own impromptu rite for them uses curds and mutton – food of the northern nomad 'barbarians', not of the Chinese. If he sells the relic, he can use the proceeds to buy a basket in which to offer sacrifices to appease the souls of the fallen. The translation is by J. D. Frodsham.

Flakes of lacquer, dust of bones,
Red cinnabar,
The ancient blood once spurted forth
And bore bronze flowers.
White feathers and its metal stem
Have rotted in the rain.
Only the three spines still remain,
Broken teeth of a wolf.

I searched this plain of battle
With a pair of nags,
In stony fields east of the post-station,
On a weed-grown hill.
An endless wind, the day short,

Desolate stars,
Black banners of damp clouds
Hung in void-night.
Souls to the left, spirits to the right,
Gaunt with hunger, wailing.

I poured curds from my tilted flask,
Offered roast mutton.
Insects silent, the wild geese sick,
Reed shoots reddening,
A whirlwind came to see me off,
Blowing the ghost fires.

In tears I sought this ancient field,
Picked up a broken arrow,
Its shattered point, scarlet and cracked,
Once drove through flesh.
In South Street, by the eastern wall,
A lad on horseback
Urged me to exchange the metal
For a votive basket.

Beowulf

In this famous epic Beowulf claims on his death-bed that the heroic code of his time has been upheld, because God cannot accuse him of the murder of kinsmen. Here he recounts an instance of 'friendly fire', in which Haethcyn shoots wide and kills his own brother. Their father's previous perspective on all his world is lost, and he dies of grief. There is reference to the ritual hanging of one who did not die in battle.

Edwin Morgan's translation gives us some sense of the manner in which the original Old English would probably have been intoned – as a kind of chant half-way between prose speech and song.

I was seven years old when the master of treasures,
Dear lord of his folk, took me from my father;
Hrethel the king kept me and guarded me,
Gave me feast and gold, never forgot friendship;
Nothing ever made me, as a child at the court,
Stranger to him than any of his sons,
Herebeald or Haethcyn or my own dear Hygelac.
The eldest brother's sudden death-bed
Was spread disastrously by a kinsman's actions
When Haethcyn struck him, his friend and his lord,
With an arrow drawn from his horn-curved bow,
Shot wide of the target, shot death to his kinsman,
One brother to another by that bolt of blood.
– Combat unatonable, conduct bitterly awry,
A breast-oppressive thought; but the prince nevertheless
Had to leave his life unavenged in its loss.
– Such is the affliction, such is the endurance
Of the grey-haired man whose own young son
Twists on the gallows; then may he keen
In a song of pain, when his boy is hanged
For the raven's joy, and his years and wisdom
Are void of power to bring him any aid.

Morning after morning he is forever recalling
His son in the far marches; he has no anxiety
To live on in longing for another inheritor
Within these courts, where one has met
Destiny's blows in embattled death.
Anguished he scans in his son's dwelling
Desolate wine-hall and wind-vexed resting-place
Wasted of gladness; heroes and horsemen
Sleep in the darkness; no harp sings there
Or happiness to those walls, as they resounded once.
He goes then his couch; solitary is his elegy
Sung for the solitary: all his castle and country
To him too empty.

– So the Weders' defender
Laboured under seething sorrowfulness of heart
On Herebeald's account; he had no possibility
Of visiting the killing on the head of the killer;
He could none the more readily harry the warrior
With acts of hatred for his little love of him.
Then in mid-grief which fell on him too sharp
He left human joy, greeted the light of God;
To his sons he bequeathed, as a man who has prospered,
His country and his townships at his life's end.

Luis Vaz de Camões (1524–1580)

From The Lusiads

*Camões, of minor aristocratic family in Lisbon, was shipped to India
in 1552 for disorderly behaviour. As soldier and official in Portugal's
Eastern Empire he wrote his epic,* THE LUSIADS, *centring on Vasco
da Gama's voyage to India in 1497–8, which marked the beginning
of direct trade between Europe and the East. By the time it was
published in 1572 the brief heyday of Portuguese domination in
Eastern waters was ending, and Camões' vigorous accounts of vic-
torious battles are counterpointed with elegiac themes. In Canto
Four, Da Gama, narrating the history of Portugal to the friendly
Sultan of Malindi on the Swahili coast, describes the battle of
Aljubarrota in 1385, when the Portuguese under King João, rallied
by the great soldier Dom Nuno Alvares, asserted their independence
from Castile. The translation of stanzas 26–44 is by Landeg White.
Note that the remarks on Castile's greed might be applied to
Portugal's conquests.*

They thronged Abrantes's city walls,
Congealed as it were by a joyous fear,
Mothers, sisters, wives, and sweethearts
Vowing to fast, and make pilgrimage.
Soon the martial squadrons arrived
Before the hosts of the enemy,
Who greeted them with a tremendous shout,
Though not a man was not beset by doubt.

Trumpets responded with the challenge,
Piercing fifes and the timbrels;
Standard-bearers unfurled the banners
In all their myriad, contrasting colours.

It was the season when, on the threshing-floors,
Ceres rewards the workers with grain;
The sun was in Virgo, the month August;
Bacchus was trampling out the sweet must.

The war trumpet of Castile sounded,
Horrifying, savage, mighty, and ominous;
Cape Ortegal heard it, and the Guadiana
Turned back upstream for fear;
The Douro heard it and the Alentejo;
The Tagus ran anxiously to the sea;
And mothers clutched their little ones fast
To their bosoms, hearing the dreadful blast.

Many faces were drained of colour
As their life blood rushed to the heart;
In great danger, our apprehension
Far exceeds the danger; or, if not,
It seems so; for the actual fury
Of attacking and vanquishing the foe
Makes us oblivious to the battle cry
As men lose eyes or arms or legs, or die.

So the uncertain battle was joined;
On both sides, the first files advanced,
Some marching in defence of their land,
Others in the hope of winning it;
At once, the great Pereira, overflowing
With valour, surged to the front of the front line,
Hacking until the battlefield was sown
With those who sought to make the land their own.

Now the charged air was shrieking
With arrows, darts, and various shot;
Under the hoofs of the foaming
Horses, the earth shook, the valley echoed;

Lances were shivered, and heavy armour
Kept crashing to the ground like thunder,
As the enemy launched their main attack
On Nuno's few, who at first hurled them back.

He saw his brothers advance against him,
(Cruel outcome) but was undismayed,
For treason against a king and nation
Is worse than killing a brother;
Of such traitors, many were present
In the front line, fighting cousins
And brothers (terrible contingency),
As in the wars of Caesar and Pompey.

O Sertorius, O noble Coriolanus,
Catiline, and you others of antiquity
Who with sacrilegious hearts became
Enemies of your native land;
If in Pluto's kingdom of shades
You are undergoing retribution,
Tell the dark king that traitors such as these
Have even been found among the Portuguese.

Our first ranks broke with so many
Of the enemy coming against them!
But Nuno was there, as a powerful lion
In the mountains above Ceuta
Finds himself surrounded by knights
Going hunting in the plains of Tetuan:
They prod him with spears and he, agitated
Prowls in his rage but is not intimidated;

He regards them grimly, but feral
Instinct and brute fury prevent him
Retreating, and he charges the thicket
Of lances even as they press on him:

So it was with Nuno, as the grass grew
Dark with Spanish blood, while
Men of his own, whose manhood he cherished,
Overwhelmed by sheer numbers, also perished.

João knew of the onslaught Nuno
Was sustaining and, as a wise captain,
He was everywhere, seeing everything,
Heartening all with his words and presence.
Like a fierce lioness, which has whelped
And ventures out hunting for food,
While her cubs, left waiting in her lair
Are stolen by a shepherd from Massylia,

In her furious roaring and rampaging,
She makes the Seven Brothers tremble:
So João, with a few, chosen men
Came charging to the front line:
– 'O brave knights, o peerless
Companions, equalled by no one,
Defend your native soil, you Portuguese!
On your lances hang all our liberties!

'You see me here, your king and comrade,
Amidst all the weapons and armour
Of the enemy, I ran to you first.
Battle on, you true patriots!'
So spoke the magnificent warrior
And brandishing his lance four times,
He hurled it, and it followed from that cast
That many Castilian knights breathed their last.

For with this, his men were fired anew
With noble shame and fresh resolve,
Attacking with re-doubled ardour,
Staking all on the game of war,

They vied: their swords smoked with blood;
Their lances pierced cuirass and heart.
They fought hand to hand, taking and giving
Blows like men oblivious to living.

Many they dispatched with cold steel
In their flesh to view the Styx.
The Master of Santiago died there
Fighting with tremendous power;
There died also, causing great havoc,
The cruel Master of Calatrava
While the accursed Pereiras, still apostate,
Died blaspheming Heaven, and cursing Fate.

Many common people of no known names
Descended along with the nobility,
To where Cerberus, with the three jaws,
Hungers for souls departing this world.
But then, dishonouring and disgracing
The pride of the frantic enemy,
The noble standard of sublime Castile
Was trampled under the Portuguese heel.

At this, battle became massacre
With deaths, shrieks, blood, and stabbing;
Such a myriad of people perished
The very flowers changed colour.
Even in flight, men died; then the fury
Dwindled, and lances were superfluous;
Castile recognized the fates were malign
Accepted them, and abandoned his design.

He withdrew, leaving the field to the victor
And happy not to have left his life;
The survivors followed, their fear
Providing not legs but wings to flee;

In their hearts' core was the anguish
Of death and of wealth squandered,
Of bruises and dishonour, and the deep offence
That others should triumph at their expense.

Some went away blaspheming, cursing
Whoever was the first to invent war;
Others blamed that ravenous hunger
That reckless, insatiable greed
Which, to possess what is another's,
Exposes wretches to the pangs of Hell,
Causes such destitution and deprives
Of sons, so many mothers; of husbands, wives.

Medieval England Rebellion

William Shakespeare (1564–1616)

The Death of Hotspur

Shakespeare's first play of Henry IV probably dates from 1596. It introduces the inimitable fat knight, Falstaff – thief, coward, wit and mentor of the King's son Hal. The rival of the prince is Harry 'Hotspur' Percy, son of the Earl of Northumberland, a romantic warrior out to 'pluck bright honour from the pale-faced moon'. Hal's moody father believes that his son is plotting to do away with him. Hal can prove otherwise. The Percies rebel, allied with the Scottish Earl of Douglas and the Welsh leader Owen Glendower. We join the decisive battle of Shrewsbury in Act V Scene 4.

DOUGLAS
Another king! They grow like Hydra's heads.
I am the Douglas, fatal to all those
That wear those colours on them. What art thou
That counterfeitest the person of a king?

KING HENRY
The King himself; who, Douglas, grieves at heart
So many of his shadows thou hast met,
And not the very King. I have two boys.
Seek Percy and thyself about the field,
But seeing thou fallest on me so luckily
I will assay thee, and defend thyself.

DOUGLAS
I fear thou art another counterfeit,
And yet, in faith, thou bearest thee like a king –
But mine I am sure thou art, whoe'er thou be,
And thus I win thee.

*They fight, the King being in danger; enter
Prince of Wales*

PRINCE HAL
Hold up thy head, vile Scot, or thou art like
Never to hold it up again! The spirits
Of valiant Shirley, Stafford, Blunt are in my arms.
It is the Prince of Wales that threatens thee,
Who never promiseth but he means to pay.

They fight; Douglas flees

Cheerly, my lord, how fares your grace?
Sir Nicholas Gawsey hath for succour sent,
And so hath Clifton – I'll to Clifton straight.

KING HENRY
Stay and breathe a while.
Thou hast redeemed thy lost opinion,
And showed thou makest some tender of my life
In this fair rescue thou hast brought to me.

PRINCE HAL
O God, they did me too much injury so
That ever said I hearkened for your death.
If it were so, I might have let alone
The insulting hand of Douglas over you,
Which would have been as speedy in your end
As all the poisonous potions in the world,
And saved the treacherous labour of your son.

KING HENRY
Make up to Clifton, I'll to Sir Nicholas Gawsey. *Exit*

Enter Hotspur

HOTSPUR
If I mistake not, thou art Harry Monmouth.

PRINCE HAL
Thou speakest as if I would deny my name.

HOTSPUR
My name is Harry Percy.

PRINCE HAL
Why then I see
A very valiant rebel of the name.
I am the Prince of Wales, and think not, Percy,
To share with me in glory any more.
Two stars keep not their motion in one sphere,
Nor can one England brook a double reign
Of Harry Percy and the Prince of Wales.

HOTSPUR
Nor shall it, Harry, for the hour is come
To end the one of us; and would to God
Thy name in arms were now as great as mine.

PRINCE HAL
I'll make it greater ere I part from thee,
And all the budding honours on thy crest
I'll crop to make a garland for my head.

HOTSPUR
I can no longer brook thy vanities.
They fight

Enter Falstaff

FALSTAFF
Well said, Hal! To it, Hal! Nay, you shall find no boy's play here,
I can tell you.

Enter Douglas; he fighteth with Falstaff, who falls down as if he were dead.

Exit Douglas
The Prince mortally wounds Hotspur

HOTSPUR
O Harry, thou hast robbed me of my youth!
I better brook the loss of brittle life
Than those proud titles thou hast won of me.
They wound my thoughts worse than thy sword my flesh.
But thoughts, the slaves of life, and life, time's fool,
And time, that takes survey of all the world,
Must have a stop. O, I could prophesy,
But that the earthy and cold hand of death
Lies on my tongue. No, Percy, thou art dust,
And food for –

He dies

PRINCE HAL
For worms, brave Percy. Fare thee well, great heart!
Ill-weaved ambition, how much art thou shrunk.
When that this body did contain a spirit,
A kingdom for it was too small a bound.
But now two paces of the vilest earth
Is room enough. This earth that bears thee dead
Bears not alive so stout a gentleman.
If thou wert sensible of courtesy
I should not make so dear a show of zeal,
But let my favours hide thy mangled face,
And even in thy behalf I'll thank myself
For doing these fair rites of tenderness.
Adieu, and take thy praise with thee to heaven!
Thy ignominy sleep with thee in the grave,
But not remembered in thy epitaph.
      He spieth Falstaff on the ground

What, old acquaintance, could not all this flesh
Keep in a little life? Poor Jack, farewell!
I could have better spared a better man.
O, I should have a heavy miss of thee
If I were much in love with vanity.
Death hath not struck so fat a deer today,
Though many dearer, in this bloody fray.
Embowelled will I see thee by and by,
Till then in blood by noble Percy lie.   *Exit*

Falstaff riseth up

FALSTAFF
Embowelled? If thou embowel me today, I'll give you leave to
powder me and eat me too tomorrow. 'Sblood, 'twas time to coun-
terfeit, or that hot termagant Scot had paid me, scot and lot too.
Counterfeit? I lie, I am no counterfeit. To die is to be a counterfeit,
for he is but the counterfeit of a man who hath not the life of a
man. But to counterfeit dying, when a man thereby liveth, is to be
no counterfeit, but the true and perfect image of life indeed. The
better part of valour is discretion, in the which better part I have
saved my life.
      Zounds, I am afraid of this gunpowder Percy, though he be
dead. How if he should counterfeit too and rise? By my faith, I am
afraid he would prove the better counterfeit. Therefore I'll make
him sure, yea, and I'll swear I killed him. Why may not he rise as
well as I? Nothing confutes me but eyes, and nobody sees me.
Therefore, sirrah (*stabbing him*), with a new wound in your thigh,
come you along with me.

He takes up Hotspur on his back
Enter Prince and John of Lancaster

PRINCE HAL
Come, brother John, full bravely hast thou fleshed
Thy maiden sword.

LANCASTER
But soft, whom have we here?
Did you not tell me this fat man was dead?

PRINCE HAL
I did, I saw him dead,
Breathless and bleeding on the ground. Art thou alive
Or is it fantasy that plays upon our eyesight?
I prithee speak, we will not trust our eyes
Without our ears. Thou art not what thou seemest.

FALSTAFF
No, that's certain, I am not a double-man. But if I be not Jack
Falstaff; then am I a Jack. There is Percy!
He throws the body down
If your father will do me any honour, so. If not, let him kill the
next Percy himself. I look to be either earl or duke, I can assure
you.

PRINCE HAL
Why, Percy I killed myself, and saw thee dead.

FALSTAFF
Didst thou? Lord, Lord, how this world is given to lying! I grant
you I was down, and out of breath, and so was he, but we rose
both at an instant, and fought a long hour by Shrewsbury clock.
If I may be believed, so. If not, let them that should reward valour
bear the sin upon their own heads. I'll take it upon my death, I
gave him this wound in the thigh. If the man were alive, and would
deny it, zounds, I would make him eat a piece of my sword.

LANCASTER
This is the strangest tale that ever I heard.

PRINCE HAL
This is the strangest fellow, brother John.
Come, bring your luggage nobly on your back.

Thirty Years' War (1618–48)

Friedrich von Logau (1604–1655)

The Dead Refugee

A Silesian aristocrat, von Logau ended up siding with the victims
of war – peasant farmers, refugees, discharged soldiers.
He wrote around three thousand epigrams and little else.
The translation is by Welsh poet Sheenagh Pugh.

What all my life I sought and could not find,
Death gives me now exactly to my mind.
I mean a house where no more death may come,
nor war, nor hunger hunt me from my home.

Thirty Years' War (1618–48)

Andreas Gryphius (1616–1664)

Epitaph of Mariana Gryphius, Little Daughter of the Poet's brother Paul

From a ceaseless procession of death in his closest family and countless deaths around him as a result of the war, the poet has chosen to draw our attention to this briefest of lives. The night Mariana was born, her home town of Freystadt burned down; the family fled and this very young refugee died on the journey.

In her translation from the German into perfect syllabic verse, Sheenagh Pugh's respect for the poet's use of strict form shines through.

I: born in flight, breathing the smoke of war,
ringed round with fire and steel, my father's care,
my mother's pain, was thrust into the light
as my land sank in angry burning night.
I saw the world, and soon I looked away,
since all its terrors met me on one day.
Though I died young, if but my days be told,
count up my fears, and I was very old.

Walter Scott (1770–1831)

Marmion's Death at Flodden

There must still be old men alive who as boys were instructed to learn by heart passages from MARMION. *Scott's enormously popular narrative poems influenced the representation of war by innumerable, inferior, nineteenth century successors. He blended the ancient Western tradition of Homeric epic with elements drawn from folk ballad and from the high-flown romances of medieval and Renaissance Europe. When he published* MARMION *in 1808, his agenda was clear. Britain was at war with Napoleonic France. His fellow Scots must overcome their ancestral mistrust of their Southern neighbours and unite with them in new deeds of martial valour. He presents the calamitous defeat and death of James IV of Scotland at Flodden in Northumbria in 1513 largely from an English point of view. Marmion is a wicked but brave English nobleman, a prototype for the attractive though sinful 'Byronic' hero invented by Scott's younger friend and compatriot, George Gordon. As a contemporary reviewer put it: 'The hero of the piece... who has been guilty of seducing a nun, and abandoning her to be buried alive, of forgery to ruin a friend, and of perfidy in endeavouring to seduce away from him the object of his tenderest affections, fights and dies gloriously, and is indebted to the injured Clara for the last drop of water to cool his dying thirst.' What overrides all in Scott's account of the battle as witnessed from a hillside by Clara and two squires is his 'epic' sense of ancient lineages from both sides of the Border clashing in fateful combat, at one of the great crises in centuries of Anglo-Scottish conflict, subject of the haunting Scots song and pipe tune, 'Flowers of the Forest'. This extract is from the sixth and final Canto.*

XXVI

At length the freshening western blast
Aside the shroud of battle cast;
And, first, the ridge of mingled spears
Above the brightening cloud appears;
And in the smoke the pennons flew,
As in the storm the white sea-mew.
Then marked they, dashing broad and far,
The broken billows of the war,
And plumed crests of chieftains brave,
Floating like foam upon the wave;
　　But nought distinct they see:
Wide ranged the battle on the plain;
Spears shook, and falchions flash'd amain;
Fell England's arrow-flight like rain;
Crests rose, and stoop'd, and rose again,
　　Wild and disorderly.
Amid the scene of tumult, high
They saw Lord Marmion's falcon fly:
And stainless Tunstall's banner white,
And Edward Howard's lion bright,
Still bear them bravely in the fight;
　　Although against them come,
Of gallant Gordons many a one,
And many a stubborn Badenoch-man,
And many a rugged Border clan,
　　With Huntly, and with Home.

XXVII

Far on the left, unseen the while,
Stanley broke Lennox and Argyle;
Though there the western mountaineer
Rush'd with bare bosom on the spear,
And flung the feeble targe aside,
And with both hands the broadsword plied,

'Twas vain: – But Fortune, on the right,
With fickle smile, cheer'd Scotland's fight.
Then fell that spotless banner white,
    The Howard's lion fell;
Yet still Lord Marmion's falcon flew
With wavering flight, while fiercer grew
    Around the battle-yell.
The Border slogan rent the sky!
A Home! a Gordon! was the cry:
Loud were the clanging blows;
Advanced, – forced back, – now low, now high,
    The pennon sunk and rose;
As bends the bark's mast in the gale,
When rent are rigging, shrouds, and sail,
It waver'd 'mid the foes.
No longer Blount the view could bear:
'By Heaven, and all its saints! I swear
    I will not see it lost!
Fitz-Eustace, you with Lady Clare
May bid your beads, and patter prayer, –
    I gallop to the host.'
And to the fray he rode amain,
Followed by all the archer train.
The fiery youth, with desperate charge,
Made, for a space, an opening large, –
    The rescued banner rose, –
But darkly closed the war around,
Like pine-tree, rooted from the ground,
    It sank among the foes.
Then Eustace mounted too: – yet staid,
As loth to leave the helpless maid,
    When, fast as shaft can fly,
Blood-shot his eyes, his nostrils spread,
The loose rein dangling from his head,
Housing and saddle bloody red,

Lord Marmion's steed rush'd by;
And Eustace, maddening at the sight,
    A look and sign to Clara cast,
    To mark he would return in haste,
Then plunged into the fight.

XXVIII

Ask me not what the maiden feels,
    Left in that dreadful hour alone:
Perchance her reason stoops, or reels;
    Perchance a courage, not her own,
    Braces her mind to desperate tone. –
The scatter'd van of England wheels; –
    She only said, as loud in air
    The tumult roar'd, 'Is Wilton there?' –
    They fly, or madden'd by despair,
    Fight but to die, – 'Is Wilton there?'
With that, straight up the hill there rode
    Two horsemen drench'd with gore,
And in their arms a helpless load,
    A wounded knight they bore.
His hand still strain'd the broken brand;
His arms were smear'd with blood and sand:
Dragg'd from among the horses' feet,
With dinted shield, and helmet beat,
The falcon-crest and plumage gone,
Can that be haughty Marmion!. . .
Young Blount his armour did unlace,
And gazing on his ghastly face,
    Said – 'By Saint George, he's gone!
That spear-wound has our master sped,
And see the deep cut in his head!
    Good-night to Marmion.' –
'Unnurtured Blount! thy brawling cease:
He opes his eyes,' said Eustace; 'peace!'

XXIX

When, doff'd his casque, he felt free air,
Around gan Marmion wildly stare: –
'Where's Harry Blount? Fitz-Eustace where?
Linger ye here, ye hearts of hare?
Redeem my pennon, – charge again!
Cry 'Marmion to the rescue!' – Vain!
Last of my race, on battle-plain
That shout shall ne'er be heard again! –
Yet my last thought is England's – fly,
     To Dacre bear my signet ring:
     Tell him his squadrons up to bring. –
Fitz-Eustace, to Lord Surrey hie;
     Tunstall lies dead upon the field,
     His life-blood stains the spotless shield:
     Edmund is down: – my life is reft; –
     The Admiral alone is left.
     Let Stanley charge with spur of fire, –
     With Chester charge, and Lancashire,
     Full upon Scotland's central host,
     Or victory and England's lost. –
     Must I bid twice? – hence, varlets! fly!
     Leave Marmion here alone – to die.'
     They parted, and alone he lay;
     Clare drew her from the sight away,
Till pain wrung forth a lowly moan,
And half he murmur'd – 'Is there none
     Of all my halls have nurst,
Page, squire, or groom, one cup to bring
Of blessed water from the spring,
     To slake my dying thirst?'

*Clare, despite the wrongs he has done her, is moved to pity and
brings him fresh water. After drinking, he repents his crimes
against her and the nun Constance. Meanwhile, a Monk has
arrived to help...*

XXXII

With fruitless labour, Clara bound,
And strove to stanch the gushing wound:
The Monk, with unavailing cares,
Exhausted all the Church's prayers.
Ever, he said, that, close and near,
A lady's voice was in his ear,
And that the priest he could not hear;
     For that she ever sung,
'*In the lost battle, borne down by the flying,*
Where mingles war's rattle with groans of the dying!'
     So the notes rung; –
'Avoid thee, Fiend! – with cruel hand,
Shake not the dying sinner's sand! –
O, look, my son, upon yon sign
Of the Redeemer's grace divine;
     O think on faith and bliss! –
By many a death-bed have I been,
And many a sinner's parting seen,
     But never aught like this.' –
The war, that for a space did fail,
Now trebly thundering swell'd the gale,
     And – STANLEY! was the cry; –
A light on Marmion's visage spread,
     And fired his glazing eye:
With dying hand, above his head,
He shook the fragment of his blade,
     And shouted 'Victory! –
Charge, Chester, charge! On, Stanley, on!'
Were the last words of Marmion.

The Monk and the Lady leave. The battle goes on.

XXXIV

But as they left the dark'ning heath,
More desperate grew the strife of death.
The English shafts in volleys hail'd,
In headlong charge their horse assail'd;
Front, flank, and rear, the squadrons sweep
To break the Scottish circle deep,
　　That fought around their King.
But yet, though thick the shafts as snow,
Though charging knights like whirlwinds go,
Though bill-men ply the ghastly blow,
　　Unbroken was the ring;
The stubborn spearmen still made good
Their dark impenetrable wood,
Each stepping where his comrade stood
　　The instant that he fell.
No thought there was of dastard flight;
Link'd in a serried phalanx tight,
Groom fought like noble, squire like knight,
　　As fearlessly and well;
Till utter darkness closed her wing
O'er their thin host and wounded King.
Then skilful Surrey's sage commands
Led back from strife his shatter'd bands;
　　And from the charge they drew
As mountain waves, from wasted lands,
　　Sweep back to oceans blue.
Then did their loss his foemen know;
Their King, their Lords, their mightiest low,
They melted from the field, as snow,
When streams are swoln and south winds blow,
　　Dissolves in silent dew.
Tweed's echoes heard the ceaseless plash,
　　While many a broken band,
Disorder'd, through her currents dash,

To gain the Scottish land;
To town and tower, to down and dale,
To tell red Flodden's dismal tale,
And raise the universal wail.
Tradition, legend, tune, and song,
Shall many an age that wail prolong:
Still from the sire the son shall hear
Of the stern strife and carnage drear,
    Of Flodden's fatal field,
Where shiver'd was fair Scotland's spear,
    And broken was her shield!

Coup d'état 2nd December 1851

Victor Hugo (1802–1885)

Memory of the Night of the Fourth

The title refers to 4th December 1851, when sporadic fighting had continued in the days following Louis Bonaparte's coup d'état of 2nd December.

LES MISERABLES and THE HUNCHBACK OF NOTRE DAME have become part of our popular culture but in France Hugo's poetry is just as well known and revered – Steven Monte's recently published translations bring the poetry back into print in English.

The child had received two bullets in the head.
The lodging was tidy, modest, peaceful, unassuming.
A blessed branch hung above the portrait near the bed.
The grandmother was there. All you heard were her cries.
We undressed him in silence. The boy's pallid lips
Opened. Death drowned out and glazed his wild eyes.
His drooping arms almost seemed to ask for support.
We found a wooden top in his pocket and some cord.
His skull was cracked open like a log that had split.
His wound was so large you could put your thumb through it.
Have you ever seen mulberries bleeding in a field?
The grandmother watched us undressing him and said,
'Look how pale he is! Come closer to the light!
His poor curls are sticking to the top of his head.'
And when we had finished, she took him on her knees.
The night was ruthless. Rifles crackled in the streets
Where the soldiers were shooting others in the head.
'You will have to cover up the child,' someone said.
Someone else took a sheet out of the walnut armoire.
The grandmother, however, brought him closer to the fire
As if to warm his already stiffening limbs.
Whatever death touches with his cold hands down here,
Alas! can't be warmed by our fires again.
She leaned his head backwards and pulled off his socks,

Then rubbed the corpse's toes in her quivering hands.
'Isn't this a sight that we aren't meant to withstand?'
She shouted. 'Sir, he wasn't even eight years old!
His teachers – he studied – said he did as he was told
And stayed alert. Whenever I had to write a note
Or a long letter, sir, it was always he who wrote.
Are they going to kill children as well now? They must
Be truly evil then. Does it not fill you with disgust?
This morning he was playing near the window outside.
To say that they have taken this little child's life!
He was passing by and they shot him in cold blood.
He was a baby Jesus, so sweet and so good.
I am old, sir: if I died, it might make some sense.
It wouldn't have cost Monsieur Bonaparte a cent
To have killed me instead of killing my child!'
She broke off, choking on her sobs for awhile.
We cried with her. Then suddenly she changed her tone:
'What am I going to do now that I am alone?
Explain that to me, each and every one of you.
There's nothing of his mother now that I have lost him too.
Tell me why they kill the defenceless and the weak.
The child never shouted, *Long live the Republic!*
We were silent, hats in hand, and could offer no relief,
Trembling in the face of inconsolable grief.

Mother, you don't understand: politics is a game.
Monsieur Napoleon – that's his authentic name –
Is poor and yet a prince. He loves his palaces.
It's fitting he has horses and valets, and always is
Providing for his bedroom, gambling and his table.
For only by maintaining all of this is he able
To save 'the family, the church, society'.
He wants to own Saint-Cloud so officials from the city
Can smell the summer roses when they come to pay respect.
This is the reason ageing mothers should expect
To use their fingers prone to tremble in the cold
To sew the shrouds of children who are seven years old.

Walt Whitman (1819-1889)

The Wound-Dresser

Walt Whitman was 42 at the outbreak of the Civil War and did not enlist. His brother George was wounded in 1862 and Whitman went to Fredericksburg, Virginia to see him. After this experience, Whitman stayed in Washington to serve as a volunteer nurse in army hospitals. It's said that President Lincoln on horseback passed the poet in the street and raised his hat.

An old man bending I come among new faces,
Years looking backward resuming in answer to children,
Come tell us old man, as from young men and maidens that love
    me,
(Arous'd and angry, I'd thought to beat the alarum, and urge
    relentless war,
But soon my fingers fail'd me, my face droop'd and I resign'd
    myself,
To sit by the wounded and soothe them, or silently watch the
    dead;)
Years hence of these scenes, of these furious passions, these
    chances,
Of unsurpass'd heroes, (was one side so brave? the other was
    equally brave;)
Now be witness again, paint the mightiest armies of earth,
Of those armies so rapid so wondrous that saw you to tell us?
What stays with you latest and deepest? of curious panics,
Of hard-fought engagements or sieges tremendous what deepest
    remains?

2

O maidens and young men I love and that love me,
What you ask of my days those the strangest and sudden your
    talking recalls,
Soldier alert I arrive after a long march cover'd with sweat and
    dust,
In the nick of time I come, plunge in the fight, loudly shout in
    the rush of successful charge,
Enter the captur'd works – yet lo, like a swift-running river they
    fade,
Pass and are gone they fade – I dwell not on soldiers' perils or
    soldiers' joys,
(Both I remember well – many the hardships, few the joys, yet I
    was content.)

But in silence, in dreams' projections,
While the world of gain and appearance and mirth goes on,
So soon what is over forgotten, and waves wash the imprints off
    the sand,
With hinged knees returning I enter the doors, (while for you up
    there,
Whoever you are, follow without noise and be of strong heart.)

Bearing the bandages, water and sponge,
Straight and swift to my wounded I go,
Where they lie on the ground after the battle brought in,
Where their priceless blood reddens the grass the ground,
Or to the rows of the hospital tent, or under the roof'd hospital,
To the long rows of cots up and down each side I return,
To each and all one after another I draw near, not one do I miss,
An attendant follows holding a tray, he carries a refuse pail,
Soon to be fill'd with clotted rags and blood, emptied, and fill'd
    again.

I onward go, I stop,
With hinged knees and steady hand to dress wounds,
I am firm with each, the pangs are sharp yet unavoidable,
One turns to me his appealing eyes – poor boy! I never knew you,
Yet I think I could not refuse this moment to die for you, if that
     would save you.

3

On, on I go, (open doors of time! open hospital doors!)
The crush'd head I dress, (poor crazed hand tear not the bandage
     away,)
The neck of the cavalry-man with the bullet through and
     through I examine,
Hard the breathing rattles, quite glazed already the eye, yet life
     struggles hard,
(Come sweet death! he persuaded O beautiful death!
In mercy come quickly.)

From the stump of the arm, the amputated hand,
I undo the clotted lint, remove the slough, wash off the matter
     and blood,
Back on his pillow the soldier bends with curv'd neck and side-
     falling head,
His eyes are closed, his face is pale, he dares not look on the
     bloody stump,
And has not yet looked on it.

I dress a wound in the side, deep, deep,
But a day or two more, for see the frame all wasted and sinking,
And the yellow-blue countenance see.

I dress the perforated shoulder, the foot with the bullet-wound,
Cleanse the one with a gnawing and putrid gangrene, so sickening,
     so offensive,
While the attendant stands behind aside me holding the tray and
     pail.

I am faithful, I do not give out,
The fractur'd thigh, the knee, the wound in the abdomen,
These and more I dress with impassive hand, (yet deep in
my breast a fire, a burning flame.)

4

Thus in silence in dreams' projections,
Returning, resuming, I thread my way through the hospitals,
The hurt and wounded I pacify with soothing hand,
I sit by the restless all the dark night, some are so young,
Some suffer so much, I recall the experience sweet and sad,
(Many a soldier's loving arms about this neck have cross'd and
    rested,
Many a soldier's kiss dwells on these bearded lips.)

Thomas Hardy (1840–1928)

Drummer Hodge

*Hardy grew up in a countryside haunted by memories of the Napo-
leonic Wars, read reports of the Crimean War as a youth, and lived
beyond the Great War of 1914-1918. By the time of the Second
Anglo-Boer War of 1899-1902, he was attuned to see the fate of one
English soldier in a huge perspective of geography and history.*

They throw in Drummer Hodge, to rest
Uncoffined – just as found:
His landmark is a kopje-crest
    That breaks the veldt around;
And foreign constellations west
    Each night above his mound.

Young Hodge the Drummer never knew –
    Fresh from his Wessex home –
The meaning of the broad Karoo,
    The Bush, the dusty loam,
And why uprose to nightly view
    Strange stars amid the gloam.

Yet portion of that unknown plain
    Will Hodge for ever be;
His homely Northern breast and brain
    Grow to some Southern tree,
And strange-eyed constellations reign
    His stars eternally.

Second Afghan War

Rudyard Kipling (1865–1936)

Ford O' Kabul River

*Kipling was an Imperialist, in so far as he was devoutly committed
to the idea that world-wide British dominion was a force for good.
But he was emphatically not a racist – read his poem 'Gunga Din' –
and within the Empire in general and the British Army in particular
his instincts put him on the side of underdogs. His imitation, in
poetry of great power, of the voices of common British soldiers,
was a revolutionary innovation.*

*Afghanistan was for Victorians a problematic, unconquerable
country where the risk was that Tsarist Russia would obtain influ-
ence, at the 'backdoor' to India. It was in this context that the
British Indian Army entered Kabul in 1879 during the Second
Afghan War.*

Kabul town's by Kabul river –
   Blow the bugle, draw the sword –
There I lef' my mate for ever,
    Wet an' drippin' by the ford.
     Ford, ford, ford o' Kabul river,
      Ford o' Kabul river in the dark!
     There's the river up and brimmin', an' there's 'arf a
         squadron swimmin'
    'Cross the ford o' Kabul river in the dark.

Kabul town's a blasted place –
   Blow the bugle, draw the sword –
'Strewth, I shan't forget 'is face
    Wet an' drippin' by the ford!
     Ford, ford, ford o' Kabul river,
      Ford o' Kabul river in the dark!

Keep the crossing-stakes beside you, an' they will
    surely guide you
    'Cross the ford o' Kabul river in the dark.

Kabul town is sun an' dust –
    Blow the bugle, draw the sword –
I'd ha' sooner drownded fust
    'Stead of 'im beside the ford.
      Ford, ford, ford o' Kabul river,
        Ford o' Kabul river in the dark!
    You can 'ear the 'orses threshin'; you can 'ear the
        men a-splashin',
    'Cross the ford o' Kabul river in the dark.

Kabul town was ours to take –
    Blow the bugle, draw the sword –
I'd ha' left it for 'is sake –
    'Im that left me by the ford.
      Ford, ford, ford o' Kabul river,
        Ford o' Kabul river in the dark!
    It's none so bloomin' dry there; ain't you never
        comin' nigh there,
    'Cross the ford o' Kabul river in the dark?

Kabul town'll go to hell –
    Blow the bugle, draw the sword –
'Fore I see him 'live an' well –
    'Im the best beside the ford.
      Ford, ford, ford o' Kabul river,
        Ford o' Kabul river in the dark!
    Gawd 'elp 'em if they blunder, for their boots'll pull
        'em under,
    By the ford o' Kabul river in the dark.

Turn your 'orse from Kabul town –
    Blow the bugle, draw the sword –
'Im an' 'arf my troop is down,
    Down an' drownded by the ford.
      Ford, ford, ford o' Kabul river,
        Ford o' Kabul river in the dark!
      There's the river low an' fallin', but it ain't no use a-
        callin'
      'Cross the ford o' Kabul river in the dark!

TWO: 1914–1945

Giuseppe Ungaretti (1888–1970)

Veglia / Watch

Ungaretti's poetry exemplifies Czeslaw Milosz's belief and fulfils his hope that 'poems should be written rarely and reluctantly, under unbearable duress and only with the hope that good spirits, not evil ones, choose us for their instrument'.

VEGLIA

Una intera nottata
buttato vicino
a un compagno
massacrato
con la sua bocca
digrignata
volta al plenilunio
con la congestione
delle sue mani
penetrata
nel mio silenzio
ho scritto
lettere piene d'amore

Non sono mai stato
tanto attaccato
alla vita

Cima 4, il 23 Dicembre 1915

WATCH

An entire night
pitched beside
a mate
butchered
with his mouth
a girn
towards the full moon
with the closing
of his hands
going right through me
into my silence
I have inscribed
letters teeming with love

Never have I
held so fast
to life

Hill 4, 23rd December 1915

Ivor Gurney (1890–1937)

The Silent One

In THE HUMAN CONDITION, *Hannah Arendt reminds us that originally (that is, in Homer) the concept of heroism did not include courage – a 'hero' was the name for one who took part in the Trojan enterprise and about whom a story could be told. The courage is in the willingness to act and speak in the first place, to insert oneself into the world, and is no less if the 'hero' is sensitive or vulnerable.*

In this poem Gurney, a composer, notes the sound patterns in speech he hears and thinks of music in the midst of battle. How does such a soul survive?

Gurney spent four heroic years in the army (he was in the battle of the Somme and in 1917 was gassed at Ypres) and fifteen years in psychiatric care.

Who died on the wires, and hung there, one of two –
Who for his hours of life had chattered through
Infinite lovely chatter of Bucks accent:
Yet faced unbroken wires; stepped over, and went
A noble fool, faithful to his stripes – and ended.
But I weak, hungry, and willing only for the chance
Of line – to fight in the line, lay down under unbroken
Wires, and saw the flashes and kept unshaken,
Till the politest voice – a finicking accent, said:
'Do you think you might crawl through there: there's a hole'
Darkness, shot at: I smiled, as politely replied –
'I'm afraid not, Sir.' There was no hole no way to be seen
Nothing but chance of death, after tearing of clothes
Kept flat, and watched the darkness, hearing bullets whizzing –
And thought of music – and swore deep heart's deep oaths
(Polite to God) and retreated and came on again,
Again retreated – and a second time faced the screen.

Wilfred Owen (1893–1918)

The Sentry

Owen, who went back to fight with his comrades in France after treatment in Britain for shell-shock and died just a week before the Armistice which ended what was then called the Great War, has become the representative figure among all 'Soldier Poets' in the English language. His general denunciations of the war are powerful – so are his stories of individual cases, like this one.

We'd found an old Boche dug-out, and he knew,
And gave us hell, for shell on frantic shell
Hammered on top, but never quite burst through.
Rain, guttering down in waterfalls of slime,
Kept slush waist-high and rising hour by hour,
And choked the steps too thick with clay to climb.
What murk of air remained stank old, and sour
With fumes of whizz-bangs, and the smell of men
Who'd lived there years, and left their curse in the den,
If not their corpses. . .
                                        There we herded from the blast
Of whizz-bangs, but one found our door at last, –
Buffeting eyes and breath, snuffing the candles,
And thud! flump! thud! down the steep steps came thumping
And sploshing in the flood, deluging muck –
The sentry's body; then, his rifle, handles
Of old Boche bombs, and mud in ruck on ruck.
We dredged him up, for killed, until he whined
'O sir, my eyes – I'm blind – I'm blind, I'm blind!'
Coaxing, I held a flame against his lids
And said if he could see the least blurred light
He was not blind; in time he'd get all right.
'I can't,' he sobbed. Eyeballs, huge-bulged like squids',

Watch my dreams still; but I forgot him there
In posting next for duty, and sending a scout
To beg a stretcher somewhere, and flound'ring about
To other posts under the shrieking air.

*   *   *

Those other wretches, how they bled and spewed,
And one who would have drowned himself for good, –
I try not to remember these things now.
Let dread hark back for one word only: how
Half listening to that sentry's moans and jumps,
And the wild chattering of his broken teeth,
Renewed most horribly whenever crumps
Pummelled the roof and slogged the air beneath –
Through the dense din, I say, we heard him shout
'I see your lights!' But ours had long died out.

George Bruce (1909–2002)

Visitations from a War-time Childhood

George Bruce was born in Fraserburgh on Scotland's north east coast into a family long established in fish processing. He was described as the uncrowned but acknowledged poet laureate of north east Scotland.

His poetry also ranged beyond this community and showed engagement with national and international issues. 'I must show in the imagination of poetry the disastrous effects on society of the misdealings of rulers and politicians', he wrote in the introduction to his collected poems.

1. Of the five waiters, white, stiff-shirt fronted
   With silver trays on the tips of fingers,
   At the ready with napkins as white
   As their paper faces,
   Four were perfect.

   The fifth had a shoe-lace untied.

   His waxwork tear at his eye
   Registered discomfiture,
   Conveyed his regret to the single customer
   In the corner.

   The naphthalene lighting placed the scene;
   Edwardian. One
   Should not shop at this restaurant
   Longer than need be
   But pass on to carnage.

2.   1914.
     He returned in 1917,
     His legs bandaged in khaki,
     His boots shining new polished.
     Marvellous how he had got rid of the trenches.

     The only reminder
     Was the thin red line at his throat.

3.   Now when big-brother Arthur
     Stepped
     Over our granite doorstep
     With his soldier's Balmoral
     In his hand

     And we had shut the door
     On the bright sea
     That customarily roared
     Outside
     And he stood there waiting

     For the mother to say
     'You're home and no different.'
     And for the jolly father
     To say
     'How many Boche this time?'

     I put up my finger
     To touch the warm flesh
     Of the hero who had
     Actually killed
     A man

     And in a good cause.

     But there was no difference
     In that hand.

That August the beaches with their waves
Sang their habitual songs.

4. O tide of no particular moment,
Mumbling inconsequences to the pink feet of little girls,
With the hot sun on the newspapers
Beneath which soft snoring fathers puff,
And the mothers knitting for dear life –
Life not yet entered on the scene
Or about to leave; content
Spilling with the sand pies on the beach,
Sporting with the swimmers in the ocean,
In the afternoon cups of tea gossiping
To the dull air; in this fixed
Security without height or depth or thought
Let the grandmothers, mothers, fathers and little children
Be no more than themselves – sufficient,
(Sufficient unto the day is the evil thereof.)
As the beach rescue throws out his chest,
As the diver cleaves the confident air,
As the billows of great Aunt Isa
Flow into and over the deck chair –
On this simple day – Hallelujah!

5. In those days
War used to be kept
Decently, as Aunt Isa said
(Like the servants)
In its place

Out there... out there.

6. 'Oot there, oot there.'
    Joe said,
    'A whale's blawn; herrin's
    There. Helm's doun.' Joe said.

    'Haud on,' Jock said,
    'Ye've cloured ma heid
    On thon damned winch;
    Watter ships at speed.'

    'Niver fecht y'r meat, lad,
    There's aye them that's waur.
    Alec got his leg aff
    Tween a gunwale an a wa.

    There's herrin oot there, lad,
    Siller for the takin:
    Whaur's the spunk in ye, lad?
    Ye hinna y'r father's makin.'

    'Muckle gweed it did ma Da,
    An him V.C. an a'.
    He mine sweeped the channel,
    But they couldna sweep his banes awa.'

7. Fortunately they recovered
    The body of the commander.
    The Union Jack fluttered a little
    As the waters enclosed the coffin.

8.   Jockie said tae Jeannie,
     'In ma wee box, in ma wee box,
     D'ya want tae see
     Fit's in ma wee box?'

     'Siller preens for lassies
     An a gowd locket for me,
     That's fit ye've got
     In your wee box.'

     'In ma wee box, in ma wee box
     's a German sailor's finger a' worn awa
     Chawed by the sharks
     Till it's nae there ava.'

     Dunt gaed the gun
     At eleeven o' the clock,
     Up gaed the rocket
     An the war's a' done.

9.   And the Lord God said,
     Can these bones live?
     For the land is full of bloody crimes,
     The city full of violence.

John Cornford (1915–1936)

A Letter from Aragon

In Edinburgh's Princes Street Gardens, a simple rock monument honours the memory of those who went from the Lothians and Fife to serve in the war in Spain. Whenever one passes, fresh flowers have been laid more often than not.

Cornford never lived to see the extent to which ordinary people in Britain would enlist. The first Englishman to join up, he arrived in Barcelona in August 1936, just 21 days after the outbreak of the Spanish Civil War. He was killed in battle on the 27th or 28th December of that year.

This is a quiet sector of a quiet front.

We buried Ruiz in a new pine coffin,
But the shroud was too small and his washed feet stuck out.
The stink of his corpse came through the clean pine boards
And some of the bearers wrapped handkerchiefs round their
    faces.
Death was not dignified.
We hacked a ragged grave in the unfriendly earth
And fired a ragged volley over the grave.

You could tell from our listlessness, no one much missed him.
This is a quiet sector of a quiet front.
There is no poison gas and no H.E.*

But when they shelled the other end of the village
And the streets were choked with dust
Women came screaming out of the crumbling houses,
Clutched under one arm the naked rump of an infant.
I thought: how ugly fear is.

This is a quiet sector of a quiet front.
Our nerves are steady; we all sleep soundly.

In the clean hospital bed my eyes were so heavy
Sleep easily blotted out one ugly picture,
A wounded militiaman moaning on a stretcher,
Now out of danger, but still crying for water,
Strong against death, but unprepared for such pain.

This on a quiet front.

But when I shook hands to leave, an Anarchist worker
Said: 'Tell the workers of England
This was a war not of our own making,
We did not seek it.
But if ever the Fascists again rule Barcelona
It will be as a heap of ruins with us workers beneath it.'

High Explosives

Marina Tsvetayeva (1892–1941)

An Officer

Here Tsvetayeva enters into the heart of a report from the war. 'The contemporality of the poet consists in so many heartbeats per second, giving the exact pulse-rate of the age – including its illnesses (NB we all gasp for breath in poems!); it consists in an extra-semantic, almost physical, consonance with the heart of the epoch – which includes my heart and beats in mine, as mine' – Tsvetayeva writing on the poet and time.

This translation is by David McDuff.

> In the Sudetenland, on the wooded Czech border, an officer
> with 20 soldiers, leaving his men in the woods, came out onto
> the road and began to fire at the approaching Germans. His
> end is unknown.
>
> From a September newspaper, 1938 – M.Ts.

The essence of forests,
Czech forestry estate.
The year: nineteen hundred
And thirty-eight.

Day and month? Like an echo, the mountains:
'The day the Czechs fell to the Germans.'

The wood's almost red.
The sky, grey-blue, clear.
Twenty soldiers are led
By one officer.

Apple-faced, his forehead sheer,
One officer's guarding his frontier.

My woods, all around.
My shrubs, all around.
My home, all around.
This is my home.

Not one tree will I give up.
Not one house will I give up.
Not one shire will I give up.
Not one *inch* will I give up.

Leaves dark overhead.
In the heart, fright.
The Prussians' tread?
Or my own heartbeat?

My woods, farewell.
My age, farewell.
My land, farewell.
This land is mine.

Let the whole land fall
To the enemy's boot.
I'll give nothing at all,
Not a stone underfoot.

The trampling of feet.
'The Germans': one leaf.
And an iron flood.
'The Germans': the wood.

'The Germans': peal cleft
Into mountain and plain.
One officer's left
All of his men.

From the wood – in lively manner –
Against the behemoth – with a revolver.

A shot resounds.
The whole wood sounds.
Wood: clapping of hands.
All: clapping of hands.

While he lashes the German with lead,
The whole wood applauds overhead.

Maple and pine,
Needles and leaves,
The whole wood's entwined,
Dense, thicketed sheaves –

By all of them
The good news is waved,
The message that's come –
Czech honour is saved.

That means that our
Land is not betrayed.
It means that war
Has been, was made.

Long live my land.
Bite the dust, Herr.
Twenty men and
One officer.

[October 1938 – 17 April 1939]

Paul Eluard (1895–1952)

Gabriel Péri

Eluard, having been the leading poet of French Surrealism, had moved by World War II towards a more direct lyrical style. He joined the Resistance to Nazi occupation, and the Communist Party. This is his plain tribute to a comrade, translated by William Alwyn.

(1944)

A man died who for his sole defence
Held out his arms to life
A man died who for his only path
Chose that where guns are loathed
A man died continuing the fight
Against indifference and death

And everything he wanted
We wanted equally
Contentment in our hearts
Light shining from our eyes
And justice here on earth
We want them still today

Words there are that make life worth the living
And these are simple words
Like warmth and giving
Justice love and liberty
Words for mild and child
And certain names of fruits and certain names of flowers
Words for courage and discovery

Comrade brother both these words are ours
And certain names for village and for country
And certain names for wife and friend
To these we add the name of Péri
Who died so we should stay alive
Remember him whose breast was riddled
His hope lives on we shall not let it end

Bertolt Brecht (1898–1956)

What did the Soldier's Wife Receive?

*Brecht, the great innovator of his time in German drama and poetry,
was in exile throughout World War 11, following the news bitterly
and keenly. This is his reaction to the sequence of Nazi conquests
ended when the Soviet Union (at horrific cost in lives) rallied and
turned the tide back. The translation is by H.R. Hays.*

And what did the soldier's wife receive
From the ancient capital, Prague?
From Prague she received her high-heeled shoes,
Greetings, good news, and her high-heeled shoes
She received from the capital, Prague.

And what did the soldier's wife receive
From Oslo beyond the sound?
She received from Oslo a little fur piece,
And the hope it might please, a little fur piece
She received from beyond the sound.

And what did the soldier's wife receive
From wealthy Amsterdam?
From Amsterdam she received a hat,
She looked well in that, the pretty Dutch hat
She received from Amsterdam.

And what did the soldier's wife receive
From Brussels, the Belgian town?
She received from Brussels the rarest of lace,
What a joy to possess the rarest of lace
She received from the Belgian town.

And what did the soldier's wife receive
From Paris the city of light?
She received from Paris a silken gown,
'Twas the talk of the town, the silken gown
She received from the city of light.

And what did the soldier's wife receive
From the south, from Bucharest?
From Bucharest she received a smock,
A strange gay frock, the Rumanian smock
She received from Bucharest.

And what did the soldier's wife receive
From the Russian land of snow?
She received from Russia her widow's weeds,
For her grief she had need of those widow's weeds
She received from the land of snow.

German invasion of Russia 1941

Nazim Hikmet (1902–1963)

from **Human Landscapes**

In 1938 at the age of 36, when Nazim Hikmet had already established himself in Turkey as the most important poet of his generation, he was arrested, charged with inciting the army to revolt, convicted on evidence that military cadets were reading his poems and sentenced to 28 years. He began writing HUMAN LANDSCAPES *in Bursa Prison in 1941 and completed the first version in 1945. It didn't appear in Turkey until 1966, after Hikmet's death. Hikmet saw his use of language as a fusion of the oral tradition of his country – intended to be sung from memory, therefore making use of the mnemonic devices of rhyme, metre, repetition – and the prose novel: a fusion which makes this epic extremely readable.*

HUMAN LANDSCAPES *has been translated into over 50 languages. Another linguist/poet duo (as with the Puranāṉūṟu translation), Mutlu Konuk and Randy Blasing, have given us this first English translation.*

Halil laid the map of the Eastern Front
    on the concrete floor of his room.
It had been pieced together from newspaper clippings,
and each part was on a different scale.
The Baltic sat right next to the Black Sea,
Warsaw rubbed shoulders with Kiev.
Orel was as far from Briansk as could be.
And on Halil's map, Moscow lay
    now a stone's throw, now half the world away.

Radio Ankara had said:
'Within ten days
  the *Fuehrer's* tanks will be rolling through Moscow.'
Halil knew that would never happen.
But not to be there in person,
  fighting to keep it from happening,
and instead to be squatting on the concrete,
with needles pricking his sick eyes
and Luminal to let him sleep
a couple hours,
to be down on the concrete
marking the latest changes on the Moscow front,
drawing with a pencil
  what they drew in blood...

A chewed-up pencil
in his dark, bony fingers, Halil
marked the latest changes on the Moscow front.
The line began at Kalinin
  and curved east
    to end above Efremov.
The front was less than seventy kilometers from Moscow –
twelve hours by foot,
ten minutes by plane
and one-and-a-half centimeters on the map.
There was no snow on the map,
  no wind,
no day or night, no life or death,
  no people.
The map was a picture,
a piece of paper.
On the map the front was one-and-a-half centimeters from
  Moscow,
and on the snow-covered earth less than seventy kilometers.
But on the snow-covered earth
bright life fought death

and the enemy
    was incredibly far away:
        as far from Moscow as the height of a new human.

The enemy reached Yakroma to the north of Moscow
    and the city of Tula to the south.
And in late November
and early December
they threw in their reserves
    all along the front.
In the first days of December the
situation was critical.

And in the first days of December,
near the city of Vereja in Petrishchevo,
the Germans hanged an eighteen-year-old girl
against a snow-blue sky.
An eighteen-year-old girl should be getting engaged,
    not hanged.

She was from Moscow.
She was young and a partisan.
She was full of passion:
    she understood, believed, and took action.
The child hanging from the rope by her slender neck
    was, in all her glory, human.

A young girl's hands felt around in snowy darkness
as if turning the pages of *War and Peace.*
In Petrishchevo, telephone wires were cut.
Then a barn burned, with seventeen German army horses.
And the next day the partisan got caught.

They caught the partisan at the site of her new target –
    suddenly, from behind, and red-handed.
The sky was filled with stars,

her heart with speed,
her pulse with her heartbeat,
and the bottle with gasoline.
She had only to strike the match.
But she couldn't.
She reached for her gun.
They fell on her.
They took her away.
They brought her in.
The partisan stood up straight in the middle of the room –
her bag on her shoulder,
fur hat on her head, sheepskin coat on her back,
and cotton pants and felt boots on her legs.
The officers looked closer at the partisan:
inside the fur, felt, and cotton was a slender young girl
like a fresh almond inside its green shell.

The samovar simmered on the table:
five gun belts, a gun,
and a green bottle of cognac on the checked cloth.
And a dish with pork sausage and bread crumbs.

The owners of the house had been sent into the kitchen.
The lamp had burned out.
The fire in the hearth painted the kitchen dark red.
And it smelled like crushed beetles.
The owners of the house – a woman, a child, and an old man –
huddled close together,
far from the world,
all alone on a
deserted mountain, fair game for wolves.

Voices come from the next room.
They ask:
'I don't know,' she says.
They ask:
'No,' she says.
They ask:
'I won't tell you,' she says.
They ask:
'I don't know,' she says. 'No,' she says. 'I won't tell you,' she says.
And the voice that's forgotten everything but these words
is clear as the skin of a healthy child
and direct as the shortest distance between two points.

The partisan
knows she'll be killed.
In the red
glare of her rage
she sees no difference
between dying and being killed.
She's too young and healthy to fear death
    or feel regret.
She looks at her feet:
they're swollen,
cracked, and frozen scarlet.
But pain
    can't touch the partisan:
her rage and faith
    protect her like a second skin...

They brought out her bag
with the bottles of gasoline, matches, sugar, salt, and bullets.
They strung the bottles around her neck,
threw the bag on her back,
and wrote across her chest:

'PARTISAN'

In the village square they set up the gallows.
The cavalry had drawn swords,
and the infantry formed a circle.
They forced the villagers to come and watch.

Two wood crates sat stacked on top of each other,
two spaghetti crates.
Above the crates
    dangled
        the greased noose.

The partisan was lifted onto her throne.
Arms tied behind her back,
the partisan
stood up straight under the rope.

Odysseus Elytis (1911–1996)

from **Heroic and Elegiac Song for the Lost Greek Second Lieutenant of the Albanian Campaign**

Before Germany intervened in the Balkans in 1941, and went on to conquer Greece, the Greeks had fought a bloody but successful campaign against invading Italians in Albania. Odysseus Elytis, a future Nobel Prizewinner for Literature, served in that war, now forgotten outside his homeland. His huge elegy for one representative Greek officer was published in 1945. The translation here is by Edmund Keeley and Philip Sherrard.

III

For those men night was a more bitter day
They melted iron, chewed the earth
Their God smelled of gunpowder and mule-hide

Each thunderclap was death riding the sky
Each thunderclap a man smiling in the face
Of death – let fate say what she will.

Suddenly the moment misfired and struck courage
Hurled splinters head-on into the sun
Binoculars, sights, mortars, froze with terror.

Easily, like calico that the wind rips
Easily, like lungs that stones have punctured
The helmet rolled to the left side. . .

For one moment only roots shook in the soil
Then the smoke dissolved and the day tried timidly
To beguile the infernal tumult.

But night rose up like a spurned viper
Death paused one second on the brink
Then struck deeply with his pallid claws.

IV

Now with a still wind in his quiet hair
A twig of forgetfulness at his left ear
He lies on the scorched cape
Like a garden the birds have suddenly deserted
Like a song gagged in the darkness
Like an angel's watch that has stopped

Eyelashes barely whispered goodbye
And bewilderment became rigid...

He lies on the scorched cape
Black ages round him
Bay at the terrible silence with dogs' skeletons
And hours that have once more turned into stone pigeons
Listen attentively:
But laughter is burnt, earth has grown deaf,
No one heard that last, that final cry
The whole world emptied with that very last cry
Beneath the five cedars
Without other candles
He lies on the scorched cape.
The helmet is empty, the blood full of dirt,
At his side the arm half shot away
And between the eyebrows
Small bitter red-black spring
Spring whose memory freezes.
O do not look O do not look at the place where life
Where life has left him. Do not say how the smoke of dawn has
Do not say how the smoke of dawn has risen
This is the way one moment this is the way
This is the way one moment deserts the other
And this is the way the all-powerful suddenly deserts the world.

Sorley Maclean (1911–1996)

Death Valley

Maclean, who was bringing poetry in Scots Gaelic into the modern era, served in the 51st Highland Division in North Africa, until he was wounded there. Translation from the Gaelic is his own.

Some Nazi or other has said that the Fuehrer had restored to German manhood the 'right and joy of dying in battle'.

Sitting dead in 'Death Valley'
below the Ruweisat Ridge
a boy with his forelock down about his cheek
and his face slate-grey;

I thought of the right and the joy
that he got from his Fuehrer,
of falling in the field of slaughter
to rise no more;

of the pomp and the fame
that he had, not alone,
though he was the most piteous to see
in a valley gone to seed

with flies about grey corpses
on a dun sand
dirty yellow and full of the rubbish
and fragments of battle.

Was the boy of the band
who abused the Jews
and Communists, or of the greater
band of those

led, from the beginning of generations,
unwillingly to the trial
and mad delirium of every war
for the sake of rulers?

Whatever his desire or mishap,
his innocence or malignity,
he showed no pleasure in his death
below the Ruweisat Ridge.

Miklós Radnóti (1911-1944)

Picture Postcards

Under the Nazi domination of Hungary, Radnóti, one of the leading poets of his generation, was sent as a forced labourer to Yugoslavia. As the Red Army advanced from the East, he and his fellows began a forced march back to Hungary under brutal guards. Radnóti himself was eventually shot because the Hungarian guards to whom he had been handed over could find no hospital to take him in, and wanted rid of their responsibility. When his body was exhumed from a mass grave in 1946, his last poems were found in his greatcoat pocket, these 'postcards' amongst them. This translation is by Edwin Morgan.

(1)

Bulgarian guns rumble gruff and wild,
pound the mountain ridge, stutter, go mild;
what a mash of men and beasts and carts and thoughts,
the road rears and whinnies, the maned sky trots.
You live unchanging within me, through this restless chaos,
you shine deep in my consciousness, forever motionless
and silent, like the angel marvelling at desolation
or an insect burying itself in rotting vegetation.

(2)

Six miles away, everything is on fire,
every house and haystack,
and peasant folk sit silent at the field's edge
smoking, stiff with fear.
One little shepherd-girl ruffles the water in the lake,
leading her ruffled flock
into the water where they drink the clouds
as they bend in their walk.

(3)

Oxen are dribbling their blood-flecked saliva.
Everyone passes blood-stained urine.
The stinking battalion stands in ragged crowds.
Disgusting death drives its fetor through the clouds.

(4)

I fell beside him, his body flipped over
as tense already as a string about to snap.
Shot in the back of the neck. – You'll end like that, –
I whispered to myself, – just lie still and quiet.
Patience spreads a flower-head into death.
Der springt noch auf, – voice above me, angry breath.
My ear stuffed with dried blood, with filthy earth.

Randall Jarrell (1914–1965)

The Dead Wingman

Jarrell entered the United States Army Air Force in 1942, but failed to qualify as a flyer and became a 'celestial training navigator' at a camp in Arizona. He learnt about the human cost to aircrew of USAAF's *bombing operations at second hand and wrote poetry of exceptional power.*

Seen in the sea; no sign; no sign; no sign
In the black firs and terraces of hill
Ragged in mist. The cone narrows; snow
Glares from the bleak walls of a crater. No.
Again the houses jerk like paper, turn,
And the surf streams by: a port of toys
Is starred with its fires and faces; but no sign.

In the level light, over the fiery shores,
The plane circles stubbornly: the eyes distending
With hatred and misery and longing, stare
Over the blackening ocean for a corpse.
The fires are guttering; the dials fall,
A long dry shudder climbs along his spine,
His fingers tremble; but his hard unchanging stare
Moves unacceptingly: *I have a friend.*

The fires are grey; no star, no sign
Winks from the breathing darkness of the carrier
Where the pilot circles for his wingman; where
Gliding above the cities' shells, a stubborn eye
Among the embers of the nations, achingly
Tracing the circles of that worn, unchanging *No* –
The lives' long war, lost war – the pilot sleeps.

Boris Slutsky (1919–1986)

The Hospital

Slutsky, Jewish, from Kharkov in the Ukraine, lived entirely in the Soviet period, and was a lifelong, loyal, member of the Communist Party of the USSR. But he was a devastatingly honest commentator on the absurdities and evils of Stalinism, and wrote about the Soviet-German war with terrifying directness. He published verse in 1941, then nothing till after the death of Stalin. His first collection appeared in 1957 and made him famous, but most of his verse was unpublishable till after his death. The translation of one of his earliest major poems here is by Gerald Smith, who explains that 'messy-smiths' translates as Red Army slang for the celebrated German Messerschmitt, Messerá, fighter-bombers.

The messysmiths still scraping through your heart,
the sharpshooters
                close by
                        still letting loose, –
our charging cheer still urging you ahead,
that Russian yell, Hurrah-rara-rara!'
– a line
        of twenty syllables,
                    no less.
A village church,
                converted into club.
Beneath production diagrams
                    we lay,
the crannies smelling still of putrid God, –
we need a country priest here, no mistake!
Anathema is strong though faith be cautious.

A lousy priest to cense away this smell!
Such frescoes gleaming in the corners!
The heavens hail!
    Halved
       with the howls
           of hell.

Down on the floor, on earth long trodden smooth,
there lies a devil,
      with a stomach wound.
Beneath the frescoes, in a clammy corner,
a knocked-out Wehrmacht corporal, on the ground.

And opposite,
      on a low trestle-bed, a youth, –
a Soviet officer, breathing his last.
His army tunic gleams with decorations.
He. Breaks the rules. Of silence.
And cries out!
     (In a whisper, – dead men do.)

And he demands, as officer and Russian,
as human being, at this extreme time
this greenish,
     red-haired,
         rotten non-com Prussian
not die here, by his side!

Stroking and stroking down his decorations,
smoothing down
      his army tunic's breast,
and weeping,
     weeping,
       weeping in frustration,
that nobody will do what he requests.

Two paces off, in his unheated corner,
flat on the ground, that knocked-out corporal.
An orderly picks up this humble man,
carries him off as far as ever he can,
that he might not
                          with his dark death
disturb the Soviet officer's
                                    shining death.
Silence comes down again.

And veterans
                  instruct
                              a new recruit:
'That's how it is,
                        that's what it's like,
                                                this war!
I see, my lad,
                    that you don't like it,
                                                do you?
So have a go
                    at fighting it
                                        your way!'

Hamish Henderson (1919–2002)

First Elegy for the Dead in Cyrenaica

Henderson's book, ELEGIES FOR THE DEAD IN CYRENAICA, *published in 1948, distilled his experiences with the 51st Highland Division in North Africa. During that time, and later in Italy, he produced songs which became current throughout the Eighth Army. After the war, at Edinburgh's School of Scottish Studies, he became one of the world's leading song collectors and folklorists.*

There are many dead in the brutish desert
    who lie uneasy
among the scrub in this landscape of half-wit
stunted ill-will. For the dead land is insatiate
and necrophilous. The sand is blowing about still.
Many who for various reasons, or because
    of mere unanswerable compulsion, came here
and fought among the clutching gravestones,
    shivered and sweated,
cried out, suffered thirst, were stoically silent, cursed
the spittering machine-guns, were homesick for Europe
and fast embedded in quicksand of Africa
    agonized and died.
And sleep now. Sleep here the sleep of the dust.

There were our own, there were the others.
Their deaths were like their lives, human and animal.
There were no gods and precious few heroes.
What they regretted when they died had nothing to do with
    race and leader, realm indivisible,
laboured Augustan speeches or vague imperial heritage.

(They saw through that guff before the axe fell.)
    Their longing turned to
the lost world glimpsed in the memory of letters:
an evening at the pictures in the friendly dark,
two knowing conspirators smiling and whispering secrets~
    or else
a family gathering in the homely kitchen
with Mum so proud of her boys in uniform:
    their thoughts trembled
between moments of estrangement, and ecstatic moments
of reconciliation: and their desire
crucified itself against the unutterable shadow of someone
whose photo was in their wallets.
Then death made his incision.

There were our own, there were the others.
Therefore, minding the great word of Glencoe's
son, that we should not disfigure ourselves
with villainy of hatred; and seeing that all
have gone down like curs into anonymous silence,
I will bear witness for I knew the others.
Seeing that littoral and interior are alike indifferent
and the birds are drawn again to our welcoming north
why should I not sing *them*, the dead, the innocent?

Corrado Govoni (1884–1965)

Lament for the Son

In March 1944, partisans attacked German troops in Rome – 33 eventually died. Hitler ordered that for every dead German, 10 Italian hostages should be massacred. This atrocity took place under the personal direction of Kappler. One of the partisans shot was Aladino Govoni, son of the poet Corrado Govoni. Hamish Henderson explained: 'just after the war I translated [Govoni's] lament for his own son. I also went to see Corrado Govoni and showed him this translation. And then, I went to see Kappler, because Kappler by that time was in captivity... I wanted to see what type of man it was, who could commit this terrible act – and found a stiffly correct, rather prosaic German who was described by his underlings as an ice-cold ambitious fanatic. I could see that that type of man was the carrier of a deadly disease.'

He was the most beautiful son on earth,
braver than a hero of antiquity,
gentler than an angel of God:
tall and dark, his hair like a forest,
or like that intoxicating canopy
which spreads over the Po valley;
and you, without pity for me, killed him
there, in a cave of dull-red sandstone.

He was the whole treasure
of war, of sanctuary and of crown,
of my accepted human poverty,
of my discounted poetry –
You, once his hiding-place was discovered
(after which no angel could sleep) –

You, with your thieving hands
that were strangers to no sacrilege,
you carried him away at the run
into the darkness
to destroy him without being seen
before I had time to cry out:
'Stop!
'Put him down!
'That is my son!'

He was my new son, he was the triumph
of my betrayed boyhood;
and you changed him, in front of my praying hands
into a heap of worms and ashes.
Mutilated, hurt, blinded,
only I know the tragic weight I am carrying.
I am the living cross of my dead son.

And that tremendous and precious weight
of such great suffering, of such unbearable glory
becomes daily harder and more heavy;
it breaks my skin,
it fractures every joint,
it tears my soul:
and yet I shall have to carry it
as my sole good –
as long as I have one beat
of love in my old veins for him.
I shall carry him, sinking on to my knees, if I have to,
until the day of my own burial.
Only then will we be down there together,
a perfect and obscure cross.

Edwin Morgan (b.1920)

'I dreaded stretcher-bearing...'

Morgan served in the Medical Corps in the North African War. This poem is 99th out of a sequence of 100 which he made out of that experience, THE NEW DIVAN.

I dreaded stretcher-bearing,
my fingers would slip on the two sweat-soaked handles,
my muscles not used to the strain.
The easiest trip of all I don't forget,
in the desert, that dead officer
drained of blood, wasted away,
leg amputated at the thigh,
wrapped in a rough sheet, light as a child,
rolling from side to side of the canvas
with a faint terrible sound
as our feet stumbled through the sand.

Patricia Ledward (b.1920)

In Memoriam

*Much of the best poetry written by British women during World War
2 remembered dead male servicemen – husbands, brothers, lovers,
sons. The poet Timothy Corsellis served as a second officer in the
Air Transport Auxiliary. He died on 10 October, 1941, aged 20.*

(TIMOTHY CORSELLIS, KILLED FLYING)

You wished to be a lark, and, as the lark, mount singing
To the highest peak of solitude your soul had found,
You wished to fly between the stars and let your song
Shower down to earth in gleaming falls of sound.

A century ago you might have done all this:
Flowers at your music would have set the earth on fire,
Mountains retained it in their hearts of rock,
In poplar boughs winds paused at your wild lyre.

World chaos coiled about you, and each upward flight
Meant struggling with the deep morass of history:
Luck was against you, poet, that you lived when guns
And tramping feet was all that mankind knew of poetry.

But solitude still called - you became an eagle.
Beneath your wings you held the slanting clouds of gold,
The earth seemed now a comic tune, for mighty orchestras
Drew you towards the sun, unblinded, bold.

A letter tells us you are dead – at twenty years.
From shocked and nerveless hands the paper slips.
We see it all – the failing engine, the numb fingers clutching,
The instantaneous fear, distorted lips,

The starting eyes, the whirling, humming sky,
The sweat of agony, the bleeding fist, the flash
Of life and panoramic view before your mind,
The whistling, screaming, downward rush, the crash.

The grass, the lonely hills, are weeping tears of green,
The sky bends low, embracing in a gentle shroud of air
Your shattered body; and the wind that sweeps the waves
Is mourning for your lively eyes and thick locks of your hair.

We, your friends, will not give way to alien tears,
But shall think in firelight of your grave voice reading verse,
Remember all your wit, your poses, and your heart
Far kinder than you'd ever have us guess.

Come! let us dance in nightclubs you frequented,
Covet with envious eyes half-breeds you wished to gain,
Thrust our hands deep in golden hair you loved to touch,
Drink till your memory ferments within our brain.

The band is changing tune to the century's Blues:
Go on, yes, dance, I'll come when I am needed –
On a far hill a youth lies dead, his mouth towards the mud,
And, like the blood, his song dissolves in earth, unheeded.

Play on, O Harlem band, O swing your blues!
Rend every stone with your terrible, lamenting cry:
Those who would sing of life, and hope, and joy,
Are driven out to hunt, to kill, to die.

WW2: The Massacre of Jewish people

Paul Celan (1920–1970)

Death Fugue

Celan was born in a German-Jewish district of Romania. His parents were killed by the Nazis, but he escaped, to become the most important poet in German of his generation. This is his most famous poem. The translation is by Michael Hamburger.

Black milk of daybreak we drink it at sundown
we drink it at noon in the morning we drink it at night
we drink and we drink it
we dig a grave in the breezes there one lies unconfined
A man lives in the house he plays with the serpents he writes
he writes when dusk falls to Germany your golden hair
     Margarete
he writes it and steps out of doors and the stars are flashing he
     whistles his pack out
he whistles his Jews out in earth has them dig for a grave
he commands us strike up for the dance

Black milk of daybreak we drink you at night
we drink in the morning at noon we drink you at sundown
we drink and we drink you
A man lives in the house he plays with the serpents he writes
he writes when dusk falls to Germany your golden hair
     Margarete
your ashen hair Shulamith we dig a grave in the breezes there
     one lies unconfined

He calls out jab deeper into the earth you lot you others sing now
and play
he grabs at the iron in his belt he waves it his eyes are blue
jab deeper you lot with your spades you others play on for the
dance

Black milk of daybreak we drink you at night
we drink you at noon in the morning we drink you at sundown
we drink and we drink you
a man lives in the house your golden hair Margarete
your ashen hair Shulamith he plays with the serpents

He calls out more sweetly play death death is a master from
Germany
he calls out more darkly now stroke your strings then as smoke
you will rise into air
then a grave you will have in the clouds there one lies unconfined

Black milk of daybreak we drink you at night
we drink you at noon death is a master from Germany
we drink you at sundown and in the morning we drink and we
drink you
death is a master from Germany his eyes are blue
he strikes you with leaden bullets his aim is true
a man lives in the house your golden hair Margarete
he sets his pack on to us he grants us a grave in the air
he plays with the serpents and daydreams death is a master from
Germany

your golden hair Margarete
your ashen hair Shulamith

Tadeusz Różewicz (b. 1921)

Pigtail

*Różewicz fought with the Polish resistance to Nazi occupation,
and emerged post war as a major poetic innovator.*

When all the women in the transport
had their heads shaved
four workmen with brooms made of birch twigs
swept up
and gathered up the hair

Behind clean glass
the stiff hair lies
of those suffocated in gas chambers
there are pins and side combs
in this hair

The hair is not shot through with light
is not parted by the breeze
is not touched by any hand
or rain or lips

In huge chests
clouds of dry hair
of those suffocated
and a faded plait
a pigtail with a ribbon
pulled at school
by naughty boys.

1948
The Museum, Auschwitz

Louis Simpson (b.1923)

Carentan O Carentan

Simpson, born in Jamaica, enlisted in the US *Army in 1943 and served with the 101st Airborne Division in Europe after D Day. Back in the* USA *he suffered a nervous breakdown, with amnesia which blanked out his memories of war. After he left hospital he began to write poetry. In 1948 he wrote out a dream he had had as 'Carentan O Carentan,' then realised that it was in fact a memory, of his first time under fire.*

Trees in the old days used to stand
And shape a shady lane
Where lovers wandered hand in hand
Who came from Carentan.

This was the shining green canal
Where we came two by two
Walking at combat-interval.
Such trees we never knew.

The day was early June, the ground
Was soft and bright with dew.
Far away the guns did sound,
But here the sky was blue.

The sky was blue, but there a smoke
Hung still above the sea
Where the ships together spoke
To towns we could not see.

Could you have seen us through a glass
You would have said a walk
Of farmers out to turn the grass,
Each with his own hay-fork.

The watchers in their leopard suits
Waited till it was time,
And aimed between the belt and boot
And let the barrel climb.

I must lie down at once, there is
A hammer at my knee.
And call it death or cowardice,
Don't count again on me.

Everything's all right, Mother,
Everyone gets the same
At one time or another.
It's all in the game.

I never strolled, nor ever shall,
Down such a leafy lane.
I never drank in a canal,
Nor ever shall again.

There is a whistling in the leaves
And it is not the wind,
The twigs are falling from the knives
That cut men to the ground.

Tell me, Master-Sergeant,
The way to turn and shoot.
But the Sergeant's silent
That taught me how to do it.

O Captain, show us quickly
Our place upon the map.
But the Captain's sickly
And taking a long nap.

Lieutenant, what's my duty,
My place in the platoon?
He too's a sleeping beauty,
Charmed by that strange tune.

Carentan O Carentan
Before we met with you
We never yet had lost a man
Or known what death could do.

Miroslav Holub (1923–1998)

Five Minutes After the Air Raid

Like other young Czechs who hated Nazi occupation of their country, Holub welcomed in principle the Allied air raids which hit Czech cities towards the end of World War 2.
But in practice... This translation is by George Theiner.

In Pilsen,
twenty-six Station Road,
she climbed to the third floor
up stairs which were all that was left
of the whole house,
she opened her door
full on to the sky,
stood gaping over the edge.

For this was the place
the world ended.

Then
she locked up carefully
lest someone steal
Sirius
or Aldebaran
from her kitchen,
went back downstairs
and settled herself
to wait
for the house to rise again
and for her husband to rise from the ashes
and for her children's hands and feet to be stuck back in place.

In the morning they found her
still as stone,
sparrows pecking her hands.

Sadako Kurihara (b. 1913)

When Hiroshima is Spoken Of

The poet, essayist and activist Sadako Kurihara was resident in Hiroshima when the atomic bomb fell on 6 August 1945. This makes her non-aligned stance in this poem all the more forceful. She seems more concerned with exposing what Wilfred Owen called 'the eternal reciprocity of tears', than with highlighting her own country's casualties.

This translation is in the traditional CHOKA form.

When Hiroshima
is spoken of, no gentle
reply may be heard.
'Pearl Harbour,' 'Nangkin slaughter'
come back in return. Others
speak out with, 'Burning to death

in Manila' – where
women and children, confined
in trenches, were set
aflame as living torches.
Blood and flame, like an echo,
return to 'Hiroshima.'

When Hiroshima
is spoken of, no gentle
reply may be heard.
The dead of Asian nations
rage in one united voice
against their violation.

Can weapons not be
discarded, military
bases dismantled?
Until then, Hiroshima
remains the bitter city
of cruelty, hypocrisy.

We are pariahs
scorched by the radiation
latent in revenge.
We must cleanse our hands ourselves
while we await the gentle
replies to 'Hiroshima.'

THREE: SINCE 1945

Ku Sang (1919–2004)

Enemy's Graves

Korean writer Ku Sang began writing poetry while a student in Japan, studying philosophy of religion. Originally from the North, he fled to the South after the liberation from Japanese rule of 1945. His poetry has a strong spiritual sense and in its apparent simplicity rejects the traditional forms of his country's poetic tradition. He published several books of verse and was also an essayist, playwright and editor.

The translation is by Ko Won.

O souls, lain asleep in lines,
would not have closed their eyes.

With our hands that pulled the trigger
against your hearts until yesterday in anger,
we have collected and buried
those rotten flesh and bones,
choosing a sunny hill, also turfed.

Death is more generous
than hatred or love.

Here, the home lands
for the souls of yours and mine,
each borders the other within a few miles.

Absolute desolation all around
oppresses my heart in bonds.

Being alive, you were related to me
only with hostility;
now on the contrary, your resentment
that you could not vent
is changed to stay with my hope.

Through the spring sky so low
clouds casually flow
towards the North.

Hearing the guns from somewhere
I burst into tears before these
graves of regret and care.

Huu Loan (b. 1916)

The Violet Myrtle Flower

Huu Loan has a long record of resistance (against French rule in Vietnam in the 1940s and against Party and government corruption under Communist rule) and leadership of Vietnamese writers and poets. He has several poetry collections to his name, including BLOODY PARADISE, *which was committed to memory during lengthy imprisonment and found its way out of the country in 1991.*

This translation by Keith Bosley was published in London when the American ground forces in Vietnam were all but withdrawn. The final three lines are from a Vietnamese folk poem.

She's got three big brothers
in the army:
her little brothers
hadn't learned to talk
when her hair was blue-black.

I'm in the National Defence Army
I'm a long way from home
I love her
like a little sister.
On our wedding day
she didn't ask for a bridal gown.

I was in uniform
with my spiked shoes
still muddy from an action:
she gave a sweet little smile
standing beside her soldier husband.
I'd got a pass from the unit:
we were married and I was off again.

From the Front far away I cast
my mind sadly back:
getting married in wartime –
how many men go and return?
Suppose I don't return:
poor wife waiting
tiny, at evening, in the country.

But it wasn't the man
in the smoke and fire who died:
it was the girl
behind the lines.
I get back
and she's not there to meet me.
My mother's sitting by a small grave
deep in a dark shadow:
the flower vase from our wedding day
burns incense now
with cold ash dropping all round it.

Her blue-black hair
was too short to tie back.
Little one! There wasn't a minute, a second
after our wedding to hear each other speak
to look at each other
once!

She used to love
the violet myrtle flower
she used to mend her husband's clothes
this coat ... once

Late one night in the jungle – it was raining –
three brothers
from the North-Eastern Front
heard that their little sister was dead
before they even knew she was married.

The early autumn wind is blowing again
thrilling the river:
the little brothers are growing up
and they look at their sister's photo puzzled.
When the autumn wind blows again
the grass is yellow round the gravestone.

One evening on an action
passing some hills covered with myrtle flowers
covered with myrtle flowers
violet myrtle flowers
violet evening, wild, vast

I see my tunic is torn.
Among the bright flowers I say the old verse:
    My hem splits:
wife I suddenly have not –
old mother hasn't sewn yet.

Nigerian coup, 15 January 1966 and October '66
disturbances following

Wole Soyinka (b. 1934)

Civilian and Soldier

When this poem was published in IDANRE AND OTHER POEMS *in 1967, Soyinka was already highly regarded as a playwright. Soyinka criticised the Federal Government in Nigeria for not doing enough to protect the Igbo people after the 1966 coup and as a consequence was detained in solitary confinement.*

Soyinka's writing, as in this poem, frequently illuminates the continuing relationship between the living and the dead.

Soyinka was awarded the Nobel Prize for Literature in 1986.

My apparition rose from the fall of lead,
Declared, 'I'm a civilian.' It only served
To aggravate your fright. For how could I
Have risen, a being of this world, in that hour
of impartial death! And I thought also: nor is
Your quarrel of this world.
　　　You stood still
For both eternities, and oh I heard the lesson
Of your training sessions, cautioning –
Scorch earth behind you, do not leave
A dubious neutral to the rear. Reiteration
Of my civilian quandry, burrowing earth
From the lead festival of your more eager friends
Worked the worse on your confusion, and when
You brought the gun to bear on me, and death
Twitched me gently in the eye, your plight
And all of you came clear to me.
　　　I hope some day

Intent upon my trade of living, to be checked
In stride by *your* apparition in a trench,
Signalling, I am a soldier. No hesitation then
But I shall shoot you clean and fair
With meat and bread, a gourd of wine
A bunch of breasts from either arm, and that
Lone question – do you friend, even now, know
What it is all about?

,

J.P. Clark Bekederemo (b. 1935)

Epilogue to Casualties

As John Pepper Clark, Bekederomo published in 1970 CASUALTIES, *a collection of poems related to the past war in Nigeria. His own Ijo people had been sucked into the contest between the break-away Igbo state, Biafra and the rest of the country, dominated by Hausa and Yoruba. This is his survey of the wreckage in what was now again 'Eastern Nigeria'. The 'fabulist' referred to is the Igbo novelist and poet Chinua Achebe, who had worked as a propagandist for the Biafran cause.*

To Michael Echeruo

In the East Central State of Nigeria, four years
After the war, I visited again the old sites
I had frequented with friends, dead
Or gone now to their own homesteads,
Admonished gently by the administrator
Of the estate for coming when reconstruction work
Was all but complete. Even then,
The ruins that greeted me on the road,
Right from Milliken Hill to the amputated
Giant astride the River Niger, raised
Before my eyes a vision of the unnatural
Disaster that is war: the bridges,
Broken before and beyond Oji,
The bellows belching again at Awka,
The skeleton carriers, camouflaged
By grass at Abagana, and of course,
The other Ogidi, strangely without

Pock-marks, hamlet of the fabulist
Who I thought would never forgive, never forget,
Knowing the wrong in his own heart.
Yet Onitsha, whether as the birthplace
Of Emmanuel Ifeajuna, Tony Asika,
Or Nnamdi Azikiwe, came as the jolt
That broke my journey to Owerri,
Aba, Umuahia, through Ulli
Ihiala which after all was but a stretch
Of road for pirate planes to spirit off
Warriors, swearing to fight to the last man
Even as they fled orphan, widow, and batman.
Here houses, scalped and scarred past surgery,
Stared at me, sightless in their sockets, like
The relics of shell-shock that they are.
One, so mutilated, it is a miracle
The parts hung together at all,
Called to me in the crush, in it one
Plump woman, careless of her bare breast
And brood, pounding yam up on a balcony,
Tilted in face of gravity. The wreck
Seemed greatest by the river, there
Voiceless and sweeping the earth as
A widow who has also buried her seeds.
To one side of her lay that giant bridge
With knee lopped in the air, while clamorous
For comfort upon her other side struggled
The old market of dreams, a forest,
Cropped of all foliage, rising already
Above two cathedral spires still in conflict
For eastern pastures, as they were before the war.

Northern Ireland conflict 1972

Seamus Heaney (b. 1939)

Casualty

This elegy from Seamus Heaney's 1979 collection FIELD WORK *commemorates the life of an eel-fisherman who used to be a regular customer in Heaney's father-in-law's pub on the shores of Lough Neagh. Heaney had often served the fisherman there when he was helping out behind the bar and on one occasion had gone out onto the Lough with him at dawn, to lift the eel-lines. This man was killed by a bomb thrown into another pub one night while there was a curfew being observed by most members of the Catholic minority in Northern Ireland – the community had come together to protest against the shooting by the British Army of 13 people at a civil rights meeting in Derry in 1972.*

I

He would drink by himself
And raise a weathered thumb
Towards the high shelf,
Calling another rum
And blackcurrant, without
Having to raise his voice,
Or order a quick stout
By a lifting of the eyes
And a discreet dumb-show
Of pulling off the top;
At closing time would go
In waders and peaked cap
Into the showery dark,
A dole-kept breadwinner

But a natural for work.
I loved his whole manner,
Sure-footed but too sly,
His deadpan sidling tact,
His fisherman's quick eye
And turned observant back.

Incomprehensible
To him, my other life.
Sometimes, on his high stool,
Too busy with his knife
At a tobacco plug
And not meeting my eye,
In the pause after a slug
He mentioned poetry.
We would be on our own
And, always politic
And shy of condescension,
I would manage by some trick
To switch the talk to eels
Or lore of the horse and cart
Or the Provisionals.

But my tentative art
His turned back watches too:
He was blown to bits
Out drinking in a curfew
Others obeyed, three nights
After they shot dead
The thirteen men in Derry.
PARAS THIRTEEN, the walls said,
BOGSIDE NIL. That Wednesday
Everybody held
His breath and trembled.

II

It was a day of cold
Raw silence, wind-blown
Surplice and soutane:
Rained-on, flower-laden
Coffin after coffin
Seemed to float from the door
Of the packed cathedral
Like blossoms on slow water.
The common funeral
Unrolled its swaddling band,
Lapping, tightening
Till we were braced and bound
Like brothers in a ring.

But he would not be held
At home by his own crowd
Whatever threats were phoned,
Whatever black flags waved.
I see him as he turned
In that bombed offending place
Remorse fused with terror
In his still knowable face,
His cornered outfaced stare
Blinding in the flash.

He had gone miles away
For he drank like a fish
Nightly, naturally
Swimming towards the lure
Of warm lit-up places,
The blurred mesh and murmur
Drifting among glasses
In the gregarious smoke.
How culpable was he
That last night when he broke

Our tribe's complicity?
'Now you're supposed to be
An educated man,'
I hear him say. 'Puzzle me
The right answer to that one.'

III

I missed his funeral,
Those quiet walkers
And sideways talkers
Shoaling out of his lane
To the respectable
Purring of the hearse . . .
They move in equal pace
With the habitual
Slow consolation
Of a dawdling engine,
The line lifted, hand
Over fist, cold sunshine
On the water, the land
Banked under fog: that morning
I was taken in his boat,
The screw purling, turning
Indolent fathoms white,
I tasted freedom with him.
To get out early, haul
Steadily off the bottom,
Dispraise the catch, and smile
As you find a rhythm
Working you, slow mile by mile,
Into your proper haunt
Somewhere, well out, beyond . . .

Dawn-sniffing revenant,
Plodder through midnight rain,
Question me again.

WWI & Britain's war in N. Ireland

Michael Longley (b. 1939)

Wounds

Like Ted Hughes, Longley writes of family members' experiences of the First World War, but for this Irish poet, war retains such familiarity with his country as to move from distant battlefields to the ordinariness of a living room.

Although full of the metrical variation of speech rhythms, the craftsmanship seen throughout Longley's poetry is still here, in the fairly strict syllabic verse form.

Here are two pictures from my father's head –
I have kept them like secrets until now:
First, the Ulster Division at the Somme
Going over the top with 'Fuck the Pope!'
'No Surrender!': a boy about to die,
Screaming 'Give 'em one for the Shankill!'
'Wilder than Gurkhas' were my father's words
Of admiration and bewilderment.
Next comes the London-Scottish padre
Resettling kilts with his swagger-stick,
With a stylish backhand and a prayer.
Over a landscape of dead buttocks
My father followed him for fifty years.
At last, a belated casualty,
He said – lead traces flaring till they hurt –
'I am dying for King and Country, slowly.'
I touched his hand, his thin head I touched.

Now, with military honours of a kind,
With his badges, his medals like rainbows,
His spinning compass, I bury beside him
Three teenage soldiers, bellies full of
Bullets and Irish beer, their flies undone.
A packet of Woodbines I throw in,
A lucifer, the Sacred Heart of Jesus
Paralysed as heavy guns put out
The night light in a nursery for ever;
Also a bus conductor's uniform –
He collapsed beside his carpet-slippers
Without a murmur, shot through the head
By a shivering boy who wandered in
Before they could turn the television down
Or tidy away the supper dishes.
To the children, to a bewildered wife,
I think 'Sorry Missus' was what he said.

Izet Sarajlic (1930–2002)

Luck in Sarajevo

The media pushes our attention from one conflict to the next, inducing a kind of cultural Attention Deficit Disorder. After the television cameras have gone, poetry brings us back to an awareness of war's lasting effects.

Izet Sarajlic was Bosnia-Herzegovina's post-WW2 best known, most popular and most widely translated poet.

In Sarajevo
in the spring of 1992,
everything is possible:
you go stand in a bread line
and end up in an emergency room
with your leg amputated.

Afterwards, you still maintain
that you were very lucky.

Igor Klikovac (b. 1970)

Festival of the Dead in a Second Division Stadium

More than 200,000 people lost their lives in the Bosnian war and more than two million people were forced to leave their homes.

Workmen mark lines on a football pitch
for an important Sunday match.
The chalky dust carried by the wind surrounds them
and rises high above their heads like ash
at a September festival in Kyoto or Osaka.

The souls of the dead are taking the best seats.

Mahmoud Darwish (b. 1941)

State of Siege (Ramallah, January 2002)

This best-known of Palestinian poets can draw listeners in their thousands when he reads (in Beirut he read for 25,000). In an early poem, DEFIANCE, he wrote: 'poetry is the blood of the heart, salt to bread, the eye's water. As such it is too important to be allowed to remain divorced from life'. Mahmoud Darwish is now living under curfew in the Israeli military-controlled zone Ramallah. In this recent poem Darwish sustains his poetic aim, to connect the daily with the metaphysical. The poem is translated from the Arabic by Ahdaf Soueif, whose novel THE MAP OF LOVE *was short-listed for the Booker Prize.*

Here, on the slopes of the hills, in front of the sunset
and the muzzle of time,
by gardens bereft of shade,
we do what prisoners do,
what the unemployed do:
we nurture hope.

A land on the brink of dawn,
we've become less smart,
as we stare at the hour of our victory:
no night in our artillery-studded night
our enemies keep watch,
our enemies light our way,
through the darkness of underground passages.

No Homeric echoes for anything here.
Myths knock on our doors when we need them.
No Homeric echo for anything ...
here a general hunts for a sleeping state
in the ruins of the coming Troy.

When the aeroplanes vanish the doves fly,
white, white. Cleansing the face of the sky
with their free wings. Regaining glory and ownership
of the air – and play. Higher and higher they fly
the doves, white white. Would that the sky
were real (a passer-by said to me between two explosions).

A land on the brink of dawn,
let us not quarrel
about the number of those who died,
here they lie together
furnishing the grass for us
that we should be reconciled.

(To another killer:) Had you left the foetus
thirty days, the probabilities would have changed:
the occupation might have ended and no memory stayed with
that infant of the time of siege,
the child would grow well, become a young man
and in some college with one of your daughters study
the ancient history of Asia.
Together they might fall into the net of love
and they might have a daughter (Jewish by birth).
So what have you done?
Now your daughter is a widow
your grandchild an orphan?
What have you done with your wandering family,
how did you hit three doves with one bullet?

FOUR: RETROSPECTIVE

US Civil War / Cold War

Robert Lowell (1917–1977)

For the Union Dead

This is the title poem of a collection published in 1961, when the Cold War intersected with the growing Civil Rights movement among people in the USA. Lowell was of patrician Boston family, but had been a conscientious objector in World War 2. At the core of this poem is the great monument in Boston to Colonel Shaw, the young white man who commanded the first black force in the Union Army which was allowed to go into combat. A very moving film about the 54th Massachussetts Regiment, GLORY, directed by Edward Zwick in 1989, starred Matthew Broderick as Shaw with a cast including African-Americans Morgan Freeman and Denzel Washington (who got an Oscar for his performance as a runaway slave). The regiment was shattered in a brave 'forlorn hope' assault on a Confederate stronghold.

'*Relinquunt Omnia Servare Rem Publicam.*'

The old South Boston Aquarium stands
in a Sahara of snow now. Its broken windows are boarded.
The bronze weathervane cod has lost half its scales.
The airy tanks are dry.

Once my nose crawled like a snail on the glass;
my hand tingled
to burst the bubbles
drifting from the noses of the cowed, compliant fish.

My hand draws back. I often sigh still
for the dark downward and vegetating kingdom
of the fish and reptile. One morning last March,
I pressed against the new barbed and galvanized

fence on the Boston Common. Behind their cage,
yellow dinosaur steamshovels were grunting
as they cropped up tons of mush and grass
to gouge their underworld garage.

Parking spaces luxuriate like civic
sandpiles in the heart of Boston.
A girdle of orange, Puritan-pumpkin colored girders
braces the tingling Statehouse,

shaking over the excavations, as it faces Colonel Shaw
and his bell-cheeked Negro infantry
on St Gaudens' shaking Civil War relief,
propped by a plank splint against the garage's earthquake.

Two months after marching through Boston,
half the regiment was dead;
at the dedication,
William James could almost hear the bronze Negroes breathe.

Their monument sticks like a fishbone
in the city's throat.
Its Colonel is as lean
as a compass-needle.

He has an angry wrenlike vigilance,
a greyhound's gentle tautness;
he seems to wince at pleasure,
and suffocate for privacy.

He is out of bounds now. He rejoices in man's lovely,
peculiar power to choose life and die-
when he leads his black soldiers to death,
he cannot bend his back.

On a thousand small town New England greens,
the old white churches hold their air
of sparse, sincere rebellion; frayed flags
quilt the graveyards of the Grand Army of the Republic.

The stone statues of the abstract Union Soldier
grow slimmer and younger each year-
wasp-wasted, they doze over muskets
and muse through their sideburns

Shaw's father wanted no monument
except the ditch,
where his son's body was thrown
and lost with his 'niggers.'

The ditch is nearer.
There are no statues for the last war here
on Boyleston Street, a commercial photograph
shows Hiroshima boiling

over a Mosler Safe, the 'Rock of Ages'
that survived the blast. Space is nearer.
When I crouch to my television set,
the drained faces of Negro school-children rise like balloons.

Colonel Shaw
is riding on his bubble,
he waits
for the blessed break.

The Aquarium is gone. Everywhere,
giant finned cars nose forward like fish;
a savage servility
slides by on grease.

Ted Hughes (1930–1998)

Out

Hughes's father, a sergeant with the Lancashire Fusiliers, survived the landings at Gallipoli (1915). 'Out' is to be away at battle but here clearly also refers to an absence in Hughes's childhood. In war, his father experienced that which lies beyond language – he had been 'buffeted wordless.'

A recording of Hughes reading this poem conveys an anger not heard in even the most visceral of his nature poems (which some have claimed also depict 'violence').

I THE DREAM TIME

My father sat in his chair recovering
From the four-year mastication by gunfire and mud,
Body buffeted wordless, estranged by long soaking
In the colours of mutilation.
                                  His outer perforations
Were valiantly healed, but he and the hearth-fire, its
     blood-flicker
On biscuit-bowl and piano and table leg,
Moved into strong and stronger possession
Of minute after minute, as the clock's tiny cog
Laboured and on the thread of his listening
Dragged him bodily from under
The mortised four-year strata of dead Englishmen
He belonged with. He felt his limbs clearing
With every slight, gingerish movement. While I, small
     and four,

Lay on the carpet as his luckless double,
His memory's buried, immovable anchor,
Among jawbones and blown-off boots, tree-stumps,
    shell-cases and craters,
Under rain that goes on drumming its rods and
    thickening
Its kingdom, which the sun has abandoned, and where
    nobody
Can ever again move from shelter.

II

The dead man in his cave beginning to sweat;
The melting bronze visor of flesh
Of the mother in the baby-furnace –
Nobody believes, it
Could be nothing, all
Undergo smiling at
The lulling of blood in
Their ears, their ears, their ears, their eyes
Are only drops of water and even the dead man
    suddenly
Sits up and sneezes – Atishoo!
Then the nurse wraps him up, smiling,
And, though faintly, the mother is smiling,
And it's just another baby.

As after being blasted to bits
The reassembled infantryman
Tentatively totters out, gazing around with the eyes
Of an exhausted clerk.

III REMEMBRANCE DAY

The poppy is a wound, the poppy is the mouth
Of the grave, maybe of the womb searching –

A canvas-beauty puppet on a wire
Today whoring everywhere. It is years since I wore one.

It is more years
The shrapnel that shattered my father's paybook

Gripped me, and all his dead
Gripped him to a time

He no more than they could outgrow, but, cast into one,
    like iron,
Hung deeper than refreshing of ploughs

In the woe-dark under my mother's eye –
One anchor

Holding my juvenile neck bowed to the dunkings of the
    Atlantic.

So goodbye to that bloody-minded flower.

You dead bury your dead.
Goodbye to the cenotaphs on my mother's breasts.

Goodbye to all the remaindered charms of my father's
    survival.

Let England close. Let the green sea-anemone close.

Battles of the Riel Rebellion c. 1885

Louise Bernice Halfe (b. 1953)

from **Blue Marrow**

In tracing the history of her own people in her long poem BLUE
MARROW, *Cree poet Louise Halfe gives a First Nations perspective
of the history of western Canada. Her imagery challenges that of
Duncan Campbell Scott (1862-1947), a civil servant in the Depart-
ment of Indian Affairs whose reputation as a poet was built mainly
on poems inspired by his contact with 'Indian' communities.*

Ripped my robes. Thrown into sea.
Spirit on their soil.

They tore flesh, breasts became pouches, hung
from their belts. Our bellies spilled.
I hung myself.

Blankets kill us. I am a large scab.

Mass graves. Fingers dig still
through the many bones.

Burned our crops. We live on mice.
We hold a Begging Dance.
Still our bellies echo.

Shot our children as they gathered wood.
Tore babies, crushed their skulls against the rocks.
The great mother sends more gods
to sprinkle water
on our heads.

The land weeps. I am choking, choking.
The buffalo are a mountain of bones.
My son is shot for killing their cow.

My canoe is swift. I become a squaw
with blood on my hands.

Let them flog.
Enter my parched land.

I am rich. Five dollar every year until I die.
Until the grass die. Until the river die.
Until the sun die. Until the wind die.

Squaw marriage. Scrounging.

My son is hung. My father became a skin
slipped through their jail like a falling star.

Duncan Campbell Scott. Captured. Barbed wire.
Squaw in mission school.

Moose milk, my joy.
I am as fermented
as the sealers in their cellar.

I will not loose my Pipe.
This holy war I stitch to my dress.
This Skull Dance, this Ghost Dance.

SOURCES AND ACKNOWLEDGEMENTS

The editors and publisher gratefully acknowledge the copyright owners of the poems included. Despite our best efforts to trace the copyright owner of each poem we have been unsuccessful in a few instances and would be grateful if these would get in touch with us (**www.luath.co.uk**) *so that this may be put right in future editions.*

Grateful thanks to De'Anne Jean-Jacques of the Authors' Licensing & Collecting Society, Alison Hanisek and Aya Ikegame for assistance with obtaining the copyright permissions. – BJ

J.P. CLARK BEKEDEREMO from *Heinemann Book of African Poetry in English*, edited by Adewale Maja-Pearce, Heinemann Educational Books, London, 1990.

BEOWULF translated by Edwin Morgan, by permission of Carcanet Press Limited, Manchester **www.carcanet.co.uk** and the translator.

BIBLE King James Version.

BERTOLT BRECHT 'What Did The Soldier's Wife Receive?' from *Selected Poems* by Bertolt Brecht, translated by H.R. Hays, copyright 1947 by Bertolt Brecht and H.R. Hays and renewed 1975 by Stefan S. Brecht and H.R. Hays, reprinted by permission of Harcourt, Inc.

GEORGE BRUCE from *Today Tomorrow The Collected Poems of George Bruce 1933–2000*, Polygon, Edinburgh, 2001, by permission of Birlinn & Polygon.

LUIS VAZ DE CAMÕES *The Lusiads*, translated by Landeg White, Oxford University Press, Oxford, 1997, by kind permission of the translator and OUP.

PAUL CELAN from *Selected Poems*, translated by Michael Hamburger, Penguin, London, 1996, by kind permission of Michael Hamburger.

JOHN CORNFORD from *Collected Writings* (1986), edited by Jonathan Galassi, by permission of Carcanet Press Limited, Manchester.

MAHMOUD DARWISH translated by Ahdaf Soueif by kind permission of the author and translator.

PAUL ELUARD from *An Anthology of Twentieth Century French Verse*, compiled and translated by William Alwyn, Chatto and Windus, London, 1969. This translation is reprinted by kind permission of the

RUDYARD KIPLING from *Selected Poems*, edited by Peter Keating, Penguin, London, 1993, by permission A.P. Watt.

IGOR KLIKOVAC translated by author with Ken Smith, in *Scar on the Stone: Contemporary Poetry from Bosnia*, edited by Chris Agee, Bloodaxe Books, Newcastle upon Tyne, 1998 by kind permission of Chris Agee.

SADAKO KURIHARA from *The Songs of Hiroshima*, Anthology Publishing Association, Hiroshima, 1980, by kind permission of the author. Translated by Miyao Ohara, Nobuku Tsukui and Beth Junor.

PATRICIA LEDWARD from *Shadows of War: British Women's Poetry of the Second World War*, edited by Anne Powell, Sutton, Stroud, 1999.

HUU LOAN from *The War Wife: Vietnamese Poetry*, translated by Keith Bosley, Allison and Busby, London, 1972.

FRIEDRICH VON LOGAU translated by Sheenagh Pugh, in *Prisoners of Transience*, Poetry Wales Press, Bridgend, 1985, by kind permission of Sheenagh Pugh.

MICHAEL LONGLEY from *Poems 1963–1983*, Secker and Warburg, London, 1991, by kind permission of the author.

ROBERT LOWELL from *For the Union Dead*, Faber, London, 1961, and by kind permission of Faber and Faber Ltd.

SORLEY MACLEAN from *From Wood to Ridge: Collected Poems*, Carcanet, Manchester, 1989, by kind permission of Renee MacLean and with permission of Carcanet Press.

EDWIN MORGAN from *Collected Poems*, Carcanet Press Limited, Manchester, 1990 by kind permission Edwin Morgan and with permission of Carcanet Press.

WILFRED OWEN from *Collected Poems,* edited by C. Day Lewis, Chatto and Windus, 1963.

PUR̲ANĀN̲ŪR̲U from *The Four Hundred Songs of War and Wisdom – An Anthology of Poems from Classical Tamil: The Pur̲anān̲ūr̲u*, translated and edited by George Hart and Hank Heifetz, by permission of Columbia University Press, New York, 1999.

MIKLÓS RADNÓTI from Edwin Morgan, *Collected Translations*, Carcanet Press Limited, Manchester, 1996, by permission Edwin Morgan and Carcanet Press.

TADEUSZ RÓŻEWICZ 'Pigtail' is taken from *'Tadeusz Różewicz: They Came to See a Poet'*, translated by Adam Czerniawski. Published by

Anvil Press Poetry in 1991. Reproduced here with permission of Anvil Press Poetry.

KU SANG from *Contemporary Korean Poetry*, edited Ko Won, University of Iowa Press, Iowa City, 1970.

IZET SARAJLIC from *Scar on the Stone*, see Klikovac.

WALTER SCOTT from *Poetical Works*, Vol. 7, London, 1833.

WILLIAM SHAKESPEARE from *The First Part of King Henry the Fourth*, edited by P.H. Davidson, Penguin, Harmondsworth, 1968.

LOUIS SIMPSON 'Carentan O Carentan' from *The Owner of the House: New Collected Poems 1940–2001*. Copyright © 2003 by Louis Simpson. Reprinted with the kind permission of BOA Editions, Ltd., **www.BOAEditions.org**

BORIS SLUTSKY from *Things That Happened*, edited and translated by Gerald Smith, GLAS, Birmingham, 1999.

WOLE SOYINKA from *Idanre and Other Poems*, Methuen, London, 1967.

MARINA TSVETAYEVA from *Selected Poems*, translated by David McDuff, Bloodaxe Books, 1987. Used with permission of Bloodaxe Books.

GIUSEPPE UNGARETTI from *Ungaretti*, Editions de l'Herne, Paris, 1968, translation © Beth Junor 2003.

VIRGIL *The Aeneid*, translated by C. Day Lewis, Oxford University Press, Oxford, 1986, by permission of Peters, Fraser and Dunlop.

WALT WHITMAN from *The Complete Poems*, Penguin Classics, London, 1986.

3 years in the making, the division of labour of this anthology fell thus: selection of the poems and Introduction were evenly shared; introductory notes to the 50 poems were 26:24 AC:BJ; the great majority of the remaining mundane but essential and very time-consuming tasks not least the indescribably complicated tracing of © permissions were done by BJ.

AC, BJ

COMBAT STRESS

EX-SERVICES MENTAL WELFARE SOCIETY

The Ex-Services Mental Welfare Society, also known now as COMBAT STRESS, was formed in 1919, after the end of the First World War. Today our purpose is to provide welfare support, treatment, convalescence and respite care for Ex-Service men and women who suffer from some form of psychiatric illness or stress disorder.

Today COMBAT STRESS has responsibility for almost 5,000 casualties of various campaigns since 1945 and has a network of twelve welfare officers and three treatment homes in Ayrshire, Surrey and Shropshire.

Hollybush House, situated six miles south east of Ayr, offers clients from all over Scotland and Ireland the peace and tranquillity of forty acres of woodland and a mile long stretch of the River Doon.

Treatment available includes both psycho educational and supportive Group work. They include topics such as: PTSD, Anger Management, Anxiety Management, Issues of Loss, Relationship Issues and Substance Misuse. Individual one to one counselling is also available. All treatment is provided at no cost to the clients.

For further information about Hollybush House contact us on 01292 560214, email hbsec@combatstress.org.uk or write to us at Hollybush House, Hollybush, By Ayr KA6 7EA.

(www.combatstress.org.uk)

Registered Charity Number: 206002

Adopt-A-Minefield®

Clear a path to a safer world

The Landmine Problem

Approximately 70 million landmines remain in the ground in 90 countries worldwide. Every 27 minutes somebody, somewhere, is killed or maimed by a landmine; as many as a third of victims are children. Those who survive endure a lifetime of physical, psychological, and economic hardship.

Local communities in mine-affected countries often do not have the resources to clear their own land and to provide adequate care to their landmine survivors, including artificial limbs, health care, and rehabilitation. Millions more people live hundreds of miles away from minefields in urban slums because their villages and land are mine affected. Economic and social development depends upon people having safe access to their land. Without mine action other development is severely impaired.

> *"Landmines are among the most barbaric weapons of war, because they continue to kill and maim innocent people long after the war itself has ended. Also, fear of them keeps people off the land, and thus prevents them from growing food. The United Nations is proud to have the Adopt-A-Minefield Campaign as a partner in the global humanitarian effort to clear landmines and raise awareness of these indiscriminate weapons of war."*
>
> KOFI ANNAN, Secretary-General of the United Nations

> *"When I was filming Tomb Raider in Cambodia I was faced with the harsh reality of the landmine crisis. I adopted a minefield in Battambang province through Adopt-A-Minefield. It has now been cleared and the people there can once again live in safety."*
>
> ANGELINA JOLIE, Actor, Adopt-A-Minefield Donor

Adopt-A-Minefield

Adopt-A-Minefield raises awareness and funds to clear landmines and help survivors of landmine accidents. 100% of all donations to Adopt-A-Minefield (UK) are applied to mine action. We are a young and dynamic charity committed to funding only the most effective mine action projects. We offer an opportunity for everyone to make a difference. It costs about £1 to clear a square metre, as little as £50 to help a child walk again. Donors are told exactly where their money has gone and receive a report after the project is completed. Adopt-A-Minefield has raised around £6.9m to date and cleared over 18 million square metres of land.

Funds raised through Adopt-A-Minefield are disbursed through the United Nations to the local and international organisations doing the work on the ground in Afghanistan, Angola, Bosnia and Herzegovina, Cambodia, Croatia, Laos, Mozam-bique and Vietnam. We've funded 26 mine clearance and survivor assistance organisations and cleared minefields in 126 villages from the 7 most mine-impacted countries in the world. We have directly benefited nearly 400,000 people by either clearing minefields in their own community or providing services such as physical or professional rehabilitation through our survivor assistance program.

Adopt-A-Minefield (UK) is a programme of the UNA Trust (Charity No. 256236) and works together with its partner Adopt-A-Minefield campaigns in the US, Canada, and Sweden. Heather Mills McCartney and Paul McCartney are the founding patrons of Adopt-A-Minefield (UK).

Adopt-A-Minefield (UK), 3 Whitehall Court, London, SW1A 2EL
Tel 020 7925 1500 www.landmines.org.uk

Some other books published by **LUATH** PRESS

Broomie Law
a collection of cartoons by
Cinders McLeod
ISBN 0 946487 99 5   PB   £4.00

*'Cinders is a great cartoonist and helps us to
see the truth behind the facade'*
TONY BENN MP

*'Broomie Law is the only thing since the
halcyon days of Steve Bell I've been
interested in buying'*
PHILL JUPITUS

*'Your work is so sharp and unusual (in these
politically surreal times), and above all,
powerful. I'm a fan!'*
JOHN PILGER

'Broomie Law is fab'
ALEX SALMOND MP

*'Broomie Law's brilliant. Just the right
lightness to drill home the point'*
GEOFF THOMPSON

'... wonderful'
GEORGE MONBIOT

*'Broomie Law is so unique and breaks such
new ground'*
DR MAEWAN HO

*'No blood but plenty of bite. And a twist of
lemon from the fact that all the characters
are female'*
AMANDA SEBESTYEN, Red Pepper

*'Cinders creations are perceptive and touch
the raw essence of today's big social issues'*
JAMES DOHERTY, The Big Issue in Scotland

'Let's get married'
JEREMY HARDY

Trident on Trial: the case for people's disarmament

Angie Zelter
ISBN 1 84282 004 4   PB   £9.99

Trident on Trial

On a beautiful summer's evening in 1999, three women – Ellen Moxley, Ulla Roder and Angie Zelter – boarded a barge moored on a Scottish loch and threw some computer equipment overboard. Sheriff Margaret Gimblett acquitted 'The Trident Three' on the basis that they were acting as global citizens preventing nuclear crime. This led to what is thought to be the world's first High Court examination of the legality of an individual state's deployment of nuclear weapons...

Is Trident inherently unlawful and immoral?

When can a state use or threaten to use nuclear weapons?

Should international law take precedence over a sovereign government's?

Can a government be held accountable for ownership of weapons of mass destruction?

When is a citizen justified in acting against what she reasonably believes to be Government crime?

Is whose name does the UK government deploy 144 nuclear warheads, each around 10 times the power of that dropped on Hiroshima killing some 150,000 people?

This is Angie's personal account of the campaign. It also includes profiles of and contributions by some of the people and groups who have pledged to prevent nuclear crime in peaceful and practical ways. Without such public pressure governments will not abide by the Advisory Opinion nor implement their international agreements to abolish nuclear weapons.

This fine book should be read by everyone, especially those who have the slightest doubt that the world will one day be rid of nuclear weapons.
JOHN PILGER

Reading this book will help you play your part in keeping human life human.
REV DR ANDREW MacLELLAN, MODERATOR OF THE GENERAL ASSEMBLY OF THE CHURCH OF SCOTLAND 2000/2001

[Un]comfortably Numb: A Prison Requiem

Maureen Maguire
ISBN 1 84282 001 X   PB   £8.99

People may think I've taken the easy way out but please believe me this is the hardest thing I've ever had to do.

It was Christmas Eve, the atmosphere in Cornton Vale prison was festive, the girls in high spirits as they were locked up for the night. One of their favourite songs, Pink Floyd's *Comfortably Numb*, played loudly from a nearby cell as Yvonne Gilmour wrote her suicide note. She was the sixth of eight inmates to take their own lives in Cornton Vale prison over a short period of time.

[Un]comfortably Numb follows Yvonne through a difficult childhood, a chaotic adolescence and drug addiction to life and death behind bars. Her story is representative of many women in our prisons today. They are not criminals (only 1% are convicted for violent crimes) and two-thirds are between the ages of fifteen and thirty. Suicide rates among them are rising dramatically. Do these vulnerable young girls really belong in prison?

This is a powerful and moving story told in the words of those involved: Yvonne and her family, fellow prisoners, prison officers, social workers, drug workers. It challenges us with questions which demand answers if more deaths are to be avoided.

Uncomfortably Numb is not a legal textbook or a jurisprudential treatise... it is an investigation into something our sophisticated society can't easily face. AUSTIN LAFFERTY

POETRY

Drink the Green Fairy
Brian Whittingham
ISBN 1 84282 045 1 PB £8.99

The Ruba'iyat of Omar Khayyam, in Scots
Rab Wilson
ISBN 1 84282 046 X PB £8.99 (book)
ISBN 1 84282 070 2 £9.99 (audio CD)

Talking with Tongues
Brian Finch
ISBN 1 84282 006 0 PB £8.99

Kate o Shanter's Tale and other poems
Matthew Fitt
ISBN 1 84282 028 1 PB £6.99 (book)
ISBN 1 84282 043 5 £9.99 (audio CD)

Bad Ass Raindrop
Kokumo Rocks
ISBN 1 84282 018 4 PB £6.99

Madame Fi Fi's Farewell and other poems
Gerry Cambridge
ISBN 1 84282 005 2 PB £8.99

Scots Poems to be Read Aloud
Introduced by Stuart McHardy
ISBN 0 946487 81 2 PB £5.00

Picking Brambles and other poems
Des Dillon
ISBN 1 84282 021 4 PB £6.99

Sex, Death & Football
Alistair Findlay
ISBN 1 84282 022 2 PB £6.99

Tartan & Turban
Bashabi Fraser
ISBN 1 84282 044 3 PB £8.99

Immortal Memories: A Compilation of Toasts to the Memory of Burns as delivered at Burns Suppers, 1801-2001
John Cairney
ISBN 1 84282 009 5 HB £20.00

Poems to be Read Aloud
Introduced by Tom Atkinson
ISBN 0 946487 00 6 PB £5.00

Men and Beasts: wild men and tame animals
Valerie Gillies and Rebecca Marr
ISBN 0 946487 92 8 PB £15.00

Caledonian Cramboclink: the Poetry of William Neill
ISBN 0 946487 53 7 PB £8.99

The Luath Burns Companion
John Cairney
ISBN 1 84282 000 1 PB £10.00

Into the Blue Wavelengths
Roderick Watson
ISBN 1 84282 075 3 PB £ 8.99

Sun Behind the Castle
Angus Calder
ISBN 1 84282 078 8 PB £ 8.99

Burning Whins
Liz Niven
ISBN 1 84282 074 5 PB £ 8.99

A Long Stride Shortens the Road
Donald Smith
ISBN 1 84282 073 7 PB £ 8.99

Scots Poems to be Read Aloud
introduced by Stuart McHardy
ISBN 0 946487 81 2 PB £ 5.00

Blind Harry's Wallace
William Hamilton of Gilbertfield
introduced by Elspeth King
ISBN 0 946487 43 X HB £15.00
ISBN 0 946487 33 2 PB £8.99

FICTION

The Road Dance
John MacKay
ISBN 1 84282 040 0 PB £6.99

Milk Treading
Nick Smith
ISBN 1 84282 037 0 PB £6.99

The Strange Case of RL Stevenson
Richard Woodhead
ISBN 0 946487 86 3 HB £16.99

But n Ben A-Go-Go
Matthew Fitt
ISBN 0 946487 82 0 HB £10.99
ISBN 1 84282 014 1 PB £6.99

Grave Robbers
Robin Mitchell
ISBN 0 946487 72 3 PB £7.99

The Bannockburn Years
William Scott
ISBN 0 946487 34 0 PB £7.95

The Great Melnikov
Hugh MacLachlan
ISBN 0 946487 42 1 PB £7.95

The Fundamentals of New Caledonia
David Nicol
ISBN 0 946487 93 6 HB £16.99

Heartland
John MacKay
ISBN 1 84282 059 1 PB £9.99

Driftnet
Lin Anderson
ISBN 1 84282 034 6 PB £9.99

Torch
Lin Anderson
ISBN 1 84282 042 7 PB £9.99

The Blue Moon Book
Anne Macleod
ISBN 1 84282 061 3 PB £9.99

The Glasgow Dragon
Des Dillon
ISBN 1 84282 056 7 PB £9.99

Six Black Candles [B format edition]
Des Dillon
ISBN 1 84282 053 2 PB £6.99

Me and Ma Gal [B format edition]
Des Dillon
ISBN 1 84282 054 0 PB £5.99

The Golden Menagerie
Allan Cameron
ISBN 1 84282 057 5 PB £9.99

Luath Press Limited
committed to publishing well written books worth reading

LUATH PRESS takes its name from Robert Burns, whose little collie Luath (*Gael.*, swift or nimble) tripped up Jean Armour at a wedding and gave him the chance to speak to the woman who was to be his wife and the abiding love of his life. Burns called one of *The Twa Dogs* Luath after Cuchullin's hunting dog in *Ossian's Fingal*. Luath Press was established in 1981 in the heart of Burns country, and is now based a few steps up the road from Burns' first lodgings on Edinburgh's Royal Mile. Luath offers you distinctive writing with a hint of unexpected pleasures.

Most bookshops in the UK, the US, Canada, Australia, New Zealand and parts of Europe either carry our books in stock or can order them for you. To order direct from us, please send a £sterling cheque, postal order, international money order or your credit card details (number, address of cardholder and expiry date) to us at the address below. Please add post and packing as follows: UK – £1.00 per delivery address; overseas surface mail – £2.50 per delivery address; overseas airmail – £3.50 for the first book to each delivery address, plus £1.00 for each additional book by airmail to the same address. If your order is a gift, we will happily enclose your card or message at no extra charge.

Luath Press Limited
543/2 Castlehill
The Royal Mile
Edinburgh EH1 2ND
Scotland
Telephone: 0131 225 4326 (24 hours)
Fax: 0131 225 4324
email: gavin.macdougall@luath.co.uk
Website: www.luath.co.uk